HILLSIDE PUBLIC LIBRARY

3 1992 00226 4324

MAY 29 2019

W9-ASC-751

HILLSIDE PUBLIC LIBRARY
405 N. HILLSIDE AVENUE
HILLSIDE, IL 60162
708-449-7510

Thinking Critically: Opioid Abuse

Christine Wilcox

San Diego, CA

Hillside Public Library

© 2019 ReferencePoint Press, Inc.
Printed in the United States

For more information, contact:
ReferencePoint Press, Inc.
PO Box 27779
San Diego, CA 92198
www.ReferencePointPress.com

ALL RIGHTS RESERVED.
No part of this work covered by the copyright hereon may be reproduced or used in any form or
by any means—graphic, electronic, or mechanical, including photocopying, recording, taping, web
distribution, or information storage retrieval systems—without the written permission of the publisher.

Picture Credits:
cover: BackYardProduction/iStockphoto.com
7: Steve Heap/Shutterstock.com
graphs and charts by Maury Aaseng

LIBRARY OF CONGRESS CATALOGING-IN-PUBLICATION DATA

Name: Wilcox, Christine, author.
Title: Thinking Critically: Opioid Abuse/by Christine Wilcox.
Description: San Diego, CA: ReferencePoint Press, Inc., 2019. | Series: Thinking Critically |
    Audience: Grade 9 to 12. | Includes bibliographical references and index.
Identifiers: LCCN 2018017507 (print) | LCCN 2018017948 (ebook) | ISBN 9781682824429 (eBook)
    | ISBN 9781682824412 (hardback)
Subjects: LCSH: Opioid abuse—Juvenile literature. | Drug abuse—Juvenile literature. | Opioid
    abuse—Miscellanea.
Classification: LCC RC568.O45 (ebook) | LCC RC568.O45 W55 2019 (print) | DDC 362.29/3—dc23
LC record available at https://lccn.loc.gov/2018017507

Contents

Foreword

"Literacy is the most basic currency of the knowledge economy we're living in today." Barack Obama (at the time a senator from Illinois) spoke these words during a 2005 speech before the American Library Association. One question raised by this statement is: What does it mean to be a literate person in the twenty-first century?

E.D. Hirsch Jr., author of *Cultural Literacy: What Every American Needs to Know*, answers the question this way: "To be culturally literate is to possess the basic information needed to thrive in the modern world. The breadth of the information is great, extending over the major domains of human activity from sports to science."

But literacy in the twenty-first century goes beyond the accumulation of knowledge gained through study and experience and expanded over time. Now more than ever literacy requires the ability to sift through and evaluate vast amounts of information and, as the authors of the Common Core State Standards state, to "demonstrate the cogent reasoning and use of evidence that is essential to both private deliberation and responsible citizenship in a democratic republic."

The *Thinking Critically* series challenges students to become discerning readers, to think independently, and to engage and develop their skills as critical thinkers. Through a narrative-driven, pro/con format, the series introduces students to the complex issues that dominate public discourse—topics such as gun control and violence, social networking, and medical marijuana. Each chapter revolves around a single, pointed question such as Can Stronger Gun Control Measures Prevent Mass Shootings?, or Does Social Networking Benefit Society?, or Should Medical Marijuana Be Legalized? This inquiry-based approach introduces student researchers to core issues and concerns on a given topic. Each chapter includes one part that argues the affirmative and one part that argues the negative—all written by a single author. With the single-author format the predominant arguments for and against an issue can be synthesized into clear, accessible discussions supported by details and evidence including relevant facts, direct quotes, current examples, and statistical illustrations. All volumes include focus questions to guide students as they read each pro/con discussion, a list of key facts, and an annotated list of related organizations and websites for conducting further research.

The authors of the Common Core State Standards have set out the particular qualities that a literate person in the twenty-first century must have. These include the ability to think independently, establish a base of knowledge across a wide range of subjects, engage in open-minded but discerning reading and listening, know how to use and evaluate evidence, and appreciate and understand diverse perspectives. The new *Thinking Critically* series supports these goals by providing a solid introduction to the study of pro/con issues.

Opioid Abuse

In May 2017 at his parents' home in Pembroke, New Hampshire, thirty-four year old Patrick Griffin overdosed on heroin four times in a single afternoon. He was revived each time by emergency services, who finally admitted him for involuntary treatment. Griffin estimates that he has overdosed thirty times over his twenty years of drug use. His mother, who is fatalistic about her son's chances of recovery, explains, "It's a merry-go-round, and he can't get off. . . . He's hurting. He's sick. He needs to learn to live with the pain of being alive."[1]

Griffin's is a typical story of the opioid epidemic. He came across opioids the way many young people do—he and his friends stole prescription painkillers from their parents' medicine cabinet and took them to get high. Griffin was already primed for addiction: a bullied child with attention-deficit/hyperactivity disorder and with alcoholism in the family, he started drinking and doing drugs at age fourteen to, as he describes, "get high and forget."[2] When the government began cracking down on opioid prescribing and pills got hard to find, Griffin switched to heroin, which was cheap and plentiful. Griffin is one of millions. *USA Today* reports that an estimated 1 million people in the United States used heroin in 2016 and more than 11 million abused prescription opioids.

The opioid epidemic has devastated communities all over America, and it shows no signs of slowing. About sixty-four thousand people died of drug overdose in 2016, more than the number of US soldiers who died in the entire Vietnam War. More than forty-two thousand of those drug overdose deaths involved opioids—a 28 percent increase over 2015. In 2017 President Donald Trump declared the opioid epidemic a public health emergency and called it "the worst drug crisis in American history."[3]

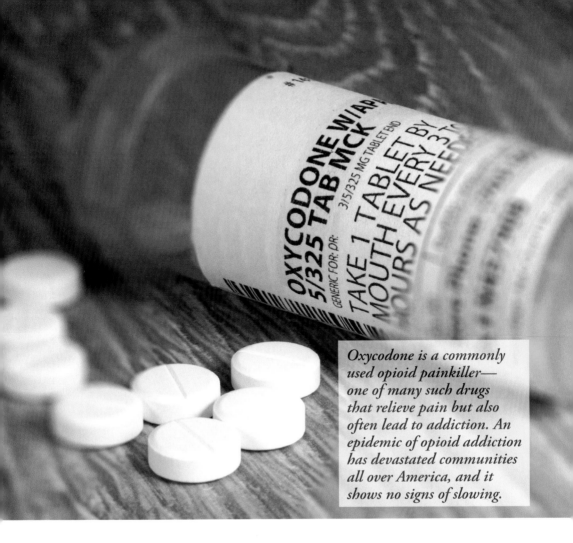

Oxycodone is a commonly used opioid painkiller— one of many such drugs that relieve pain but also often lead to addiction. An epidemic of opioid addiction has devastated communities all over America, and it shows no signs of slowing.

Why Opioids Are So Addictive

Opioids are a group of drugs with similar molecular structures that are used to relieve pain. They include heroin, fentanyl (a prescription painkiller that is easily made in illegal labs), morphine, methadone, and commonly prescribed painkillers like oxycodone, hydrocodone, and codeine. While each of these opioids has different strengths, they all work in essentially the same way: They hijack the parts of the brain that regulate both pain and euphoria. When taken in large doses, they create pleasure far more powerful than the body can produce on its own.

This pleasure can trigger addiction in vulnerable individuals. Opioids are so powerful that they can rewire the brain's dopamine system—a system that helps humans remember and repeat satisfying experiences. For example, children clamor for ice cream because of dopamine; when dopamine is triggered (by the sight of the ice-cream shop), it creates emotions like anticipation, craving, and desire. Unfortunately, the pleasure from opioids is so intense that, if repeated often enough, craving and desire overwhelm the brain, overriding rational thought and self-preservation.

Opioid addiction is deadly because users develop tolerance to the drug—that is, they need more and more of it to experience the same level of pleasure. Christopher Caldwell describes the power of addiction and the danger of opioid tolerance in his notable article on the subject, "American Carnage":

> The drug sets an addictive trap that is sinister and subtle. It provides a euphoria—a feeling of contentment, simplification, and release—which users swear has no equal. Users quickly develop a tolerance, requiring higher and higher amounts to get the same effect. The dosage required to attain the feeling the user originally experienced rises until it is higher than the dosage that will kill him. . . . If a heroin addict sees on the news that a user or two has died from an overly strong batch of heroin in some housing project somewhere, his first thought is, "Where is that? That's the stuff I want."[4]

Opioids kill by depressing the central nervous system—people who die from overdose simply stop breathing. This is almost always accidental. It frequently happens when addicts mix opioids with other drugs that also suppress the central nervous system (such as alcohol or sleeping pills). It also happens when the opioid is much stronger than the addict realizes. Many illicit drug manufacturers mix fentanyl into their products, which can be up to one hundred times more powerful than heroin or oxycodone. Just a few grains of fentanyl can kill. The Centers for Disease Control and Prevention (CDC) reports that in 2016, about twenty thousand deaths—or almost half of all opioid-related deaths—involved fentanyl. In hard-hit states like New Hampshire, where Griffin lives, 70 percent of all overdose deaths involved fentanyl.

From Pain Pills to Heroin

The opioid epidemic began in the mid-1990s, when the medical community began aggressively treating chronic pain with opioids like Percocet and OxyContin. Some doctors acted unethically, setting up pain clinics and distributing prescriptions indiscriminately, and some pain patients got addicted. However, most cases of addiction were due to diversion—a term that refers to the transfer of prescription drugs to another person for illicit use. As Caldwell describes, once these drugs were readily available in the general population, "the supply 'found' people susceptible to addiction. . . . A person who would never have become a heroin addict . . . could now become the equivalent of one, in a more antiseptic way."[5]

> "A person who would never have become a heroin addict . . . could now become the equivalent of one, in a more antiseptic way."[5]
>
> —Christopher Caldwell, author of "American Carnage"

One such person was Matt Ganem, who discovered opioids as a youth in Long Island, New York. "We were doing [OxyContin] on the weekends, we were doing it at parties,"[6] he explains. He assumed the pills were relatively harmless—not like heroin, which most people associated with inner-city crime, poverty, and death. But soon Ganem's life revolved around getting his daily dose of OxyContin. When he could not afford his pills anymore, his body was wracked with horrible withdrawal symptoms, like anxiety, intense body aches, and violent diarrhea. "It's pure agony," he says. "I was dope sick off of Oxys, curled up like a baby and I couldn't afford another pill. Somebody brought a bag of heroin to me and at that point it didn't matter what it was, I was so sick. I just didn't want to be sick."[7] Like many people who had become addicted to painkillers, Ganem became a heroin addict.

Addiction Versus Physical Dependence

Many people wrongly believe that addiction and physical dependence are one and the same. This is not true. For instance, Ganem's withdrawal symptoms were a predictable result of physical dependence; when he stopped taking opioids, his body had a physical reaction. "Dependence and physical withdrawal symptoms are the body's reaction to opioid medications and have nothing to do with mental weakness, will power or lack of character," explains addiction specialist Dr. Stacy Seikel. "Almost all patients who use an opioid pain medication . . . for more than a month will experience physical withdrawal symptoms when they stop taking the medication."[8] Such withdrawal symptoms constitute dependence.

However, Ganem was also an addict. Opioids triggered a disease process in his brain that caused him to obsessively seek the drug, regardless of how much it harmed him. Many things make a person vulnerable to the disease of addiction, such as genetics, low dopamine levels, mental illness, poverty, and psychological pain. The euphoria that opioids provide can impact vulnerable individuals so powerfully that the disease process is triggered.

Although painful, withdrawal due to opioid dependence lasts only a few days. Addiction, however, causes changes in the brain that can be permanent. Many experts report that it can take years before an addict's brain reaches equilibrium and cravings subside enough for normal life to resume. Even then, the risk of relapse will always be there. Most addiction doctors say that almost every addict who enters a treatment program can expect to relapse at least once.

Treating Opioid Addiction

While there is much debate about how to combat the opioid epidemic, nearly everyone agrees that treatment for addiction is the only way to help the millions of people currently addicted to opioids. Many addiction experts believe strongly in medication-assisted treatment, or MAT. One popular but controversial medication used in MAT is buprenorphine, a mild opioid that can ease an addict's withdrawal symptoms. "We need to get people stabilized, and restore their brain to normal function so they are able to think normally,"[9] explains substance abuse specialist Dr. Sarah Wakeman. Others are skeptical of MAT, arguing that it simply replaces one drug with another.

There also is no agreement about how treatment should be paid for. Inpatient treatment can cost upward of $50,000 per month—a figure out of reach for people without insurance. In addition, many treatment centers have long waiting lists. For this reason, states are asking the federal government for money to fund treatment centers and develop new MATs to make treatment more effective.

The opioid epidemic is perhaps the greatest health care challenge in US history. Epidemiologist Brandon Marshall of Brown University estimates that if nothing is done, the death rate from overdose will top one hundred thousand per year by 2025. The United States must find a way to stop new incidences of addiction and treat those already addicted if it hopes to end the epidemic. Unfortunately, so far, there is no clear solution.

Chapter One

Should Opioids Be Used to Treat Chronic Pain?

Opioids Are Necessary for People in Chronic Pain

- Chronic pain is a disease, and doctors are ethically obligated to treat it.
- When taken as prescribed, opioids are a safe and effective treatment for chronic pain.
- Pain patients who lose access to their prescription painkillers can experience levels of pain that destroy their quality of life and lead them to consider or commit suicide.
- Because of misplaced fear of addiction, some pain patients refuse to take opioids and suffer unnecessarily.

The Debate at a Glance

Opioids Are Not an Effective Solution for Chronic Pain

- Opioids are not the best way to control many types of chronic pain.
- Over time, opioids can cause an increased sensitivity to pain.
- Long-term opioid treatment reduces the ability to function and quality of life in many pain patients.
- For back pain and arthritis, opioids are no more effective than over-the-counter painkillers.

Opioids Are Necessary for People in Chronic Pain

"The reality is that for millions of people with chronic pain, opioid therapy is effective and safe in helping them to live more comfortable and productive lives."

—Addiction specialist Dr. Charles Argoff

Charles Argoff, "Conflating Effective Chronic Pain Management and Opioid Abuse Potential," Medscape, April 14, 2017. www.medscape.com.

Consider these questions as you read:

1. Do you think chronic pain patients should be permitted to take high doses of opioids? Why or why not?
2. This article takes the point of view that chronic pain is a disease, not a symptom. Do you agree? Why or why not?
3. How persuasive is the argument that opioids are safe? Use examples from the text in your answer.

Editor's note: The discussion that follows presents common arguments made in support of this perspective, reinforced by facts, quotes, and examples taken from various sources.

John Nolte's wife has trigeminal neuralgia, a disorder that causes intense pain in the trigeminal facial nerve. "They call it the suicide disease for a reason," Nolte writes. "Up to 25 percent of sufferers take their own lives as a means to escape what [has been described] as 'one of the most painful afflictions known to mankind.'" For years, Nolte's wife had excruciating pain in her face. "The pain in her teeth was so intense, brushing was unbearable," he says. "She could only (barely) eat soft foods. Applying make-up, even a powder, was pure agony. And those were the good days, the days when she could at least barely function." Nolte's wife finally found relief through a combination of a nerve stimulator implant and powerful doses of opioids. The possibility that his wife would become addicted to the drugs was the least of their concerns. "When the pain is this real, there is no high, no lift, no euphoria, and no concern about addiction," Nolte says. "To us, these opioids are miracle drugs, magic pills that gave us our normal life back."[10]

Opioids truly are "miracle drugs" for people who live in constant pain. According to the World Institute of Pain, "Opioid therapy is an established, effective therapy option for many people with chronic pain."[11] Opioids help burn victims and people with catastrophic injuries bear long months of painful healing and help relax muscles so that healing can occur. They also give people with intractable pain—pain with no cure—their lives back. Taken as prescribed, opioids are safe and have a low incidence of addiction. And they are necessary. According to the International Pain Foundation (iPain), an estimated 50 million to 100 million people in the United States suffer from chronic pain, which has devastating personal and economic impacts. iPain's core belief is one that all doctors should share: "Allowing people to suffer with unmanaged pain is immoral and unethical."[12]

> "To us, these opioids are miracle drugs, magic pills that gave us our normal life back."[10]
>
> —John Nolte, whose wife suffers from chronic pain

The current backlash against prescription opioids—a reaction to an epidemic of illicit opioid use—is destroying the lives of people like the Noltes, who can no longer obtain the correct dosage of these miracle drugs. Despite the potential for abuse, society must realize that opioids are the best treatment for many types of chronic pain.

When Used as Prescribed, Opioids Are Safe

It is well established that when taken as prescribed, opioids are safe. "Long-term use of opioids, unlike alcohol, really doesn't have deleterious effects on the body," explains Dr. Jeffrey Singer. "That's why we place people on methadone maintenance, for example, sometimes for their whole lives."[13] The real danger of opioids is overdose. But doctors are trained not to prescribe opioids at levels that will cause patients to overdose—and the few doctors who have done so have gone to jail. In short, overdose simply does not happen if opioids are taken as prescribed. It happens when these drugs are abused, used illicitly, or combined with other drugs. For instance, according to a 2016 study by the CDC, over three-quarters of overdose deaths that involved oxycodone and hydrocodone (the most commonly prescribed opioids) also involved other drugs.

In addition, the idea that most pain patients get addicted to their pain medication is a myth. Some do—especially those with underlying addiction issues—but the numbers are extremely low. According to the *CDC Guideline for Prescribing Opioids for Chronic Pain—United States, 2016*, research has found that, on average, only 6.1 percent of chronic pain patients on high-dose opioid therapy become addicted to their medication. For patients taking low doses, only 0.7 percent develop an addiction. Meanwhile, the very few pain patients who die from overdose usually have transitioned to heroin or illicit fentanyl—which together cause the majority of overdose deaths in the United States. This also is very uncommon. According to Dr. Nora D. Volkow and psychologist A. Thomas McLellan, only about 4 percent of people addicted to prescription opioids transition to heroin, "mainly because heroin is typically cheaper and in some instances easier to obtain than opioids."[14]

> **"Allowing people to suffer with unmanaged pain is immoral and unethical."**[12]
>
> —iPain

Opioids Allow Pain Patients to Live Normal Lives

Chronic pain is not just a symptom; it is a disease. According to iPain, "Chronic pain is a real and complex disease that exists either by itself or it can be linked with other medical conditions."[15] This has been established by the International Association for the Study of Pain, a highly respected organization that promotes pain research and education. In 2001 the association formally declared that chronic pain is "a major healthcare problem, [and] a disease in its own right." The group states, "Chronic

Undermedicated Pain Patients Suffer Unnecessarily

In 2017 the Pain News Network conducted a survey of over three thousand pain patients to see how the national effort to reduce opioid prescribing was affecting them. The vast majority of patients said that their pain had increased because their opioid prescription had been reduced or eliminated, and almost half said they had considered suicide to escape chronic pain. This strongly supports the idea that many pain patients need opioids to control their pain and maintain quality of life.

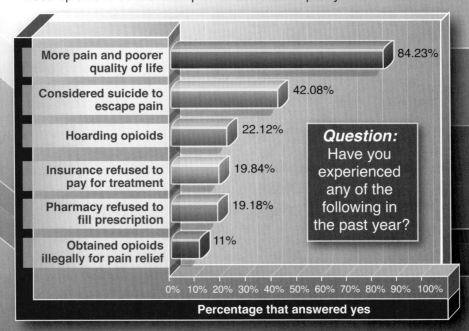

More pain and poorer quality of life	84.23%
Considered suicide to escape pain	42.08%
Hoarding opioids	22.12%
Insurance refused to pay for treatment	19.84%
Pharmacy refused to fill prescription	19.18%
Obtained opioids illegally for pain relief	11%

Question: Have you experienced any of the following in the past year?

0% 10% 20% 30% 40% 50% 60% 70% 80% 90% 100%

Percentage that answered yes

Source: Pain News Network, "2017 CDC Survey Results," 2018. www.painnewsnetwork.org.

pain often sets the stage for the emergence of a complex set of physical and psychosocial changes . . . that add greatly to the burden of the pain patient."[16] Some of these include immobility and physical degeneration, disturbed sleep, poor appetite and nutrition, depression of the immune system, inability to work, overdependence on family, isolation, anxiety, depression, and suicide.

For many people suffering with the disease of chronic pain, high doses of opioids are the only way they find relief and lead a normal life. For instance, Mr. Haller successfully used prescription opioids to manage his fibromyalgia—a disease of the nervous system that causes debilitating muscle pain. Then Mr. Haller's insurance company decided it would pay for only one-quarter of his prescribed dosage—leaving the Hallers with about $1,000 in out-of-pocket costs, which the Hallers could not afford. "If they're cutting him back all the way to this, he's not going to be able to function," Mrs. Haller says. "They're cutting [pain patients] back so bad that they're going to want to kill themselves."[17] Tamara Walker also had her prescription reduced. Walker had broken her back in five places in a car crash several years before. "I wouldn't wish this pain on anyone," she says. "And I'm afraid of the amount of pain I could feel, because I know what it's like when I don't take anything at all."[18]

Patients like Walker and Mr. Haller have had their lives destroyed when their opioid prescriptions are reduced or eliminated. They even start acting like stereotypical addicts, hoarding medication and worrying about how they will get their next dose. But their aim is not to get high, and they are not addicted—they are just afraid of debilitating, unbearable pain. They are also at increased risk of suicide. While there is no official data about the suicide rate among chronic pain patients, experts believe it is roughly twice the rate of the general population. This means that as many as twenty thousand or more chronic pain sufferers kill themselves each year.

When Pain Patients Fear Opioid Addiction, They Suffer

The myth that pain patients get addicted to their medication has made some people fear addiction so much that they suffer unnecessarily. For instance, Paul, a sixty-three-year-old man living with degenerative nerve disease, has constant pain in his legs and is unable to walk more than a few steps at a time. "He's got Percocet, but he won't take it because he thinks he'll get addicted," his wife says. "So he's miserable all the time, and says his life is over."[19] Mary, a seventy-eight-year-old woman with end-stage cancer, will not take her painkillers either. "I am not going to become a drug addict," she told her daughter. "I've never touched drugs and I never will."[20] Both Paul and Mary have an extremely reduced quality of life, even though effective drugs exist that could ease their suffering.

Opioid addiction is not a significant problem among chronic pain patients. However, denying that opioids are effective at controlling pain and vilifying the doctors who prescribe them leads to suffering for chronic pain patients. Opioids are miracle drugs that can give pain patients their lives back. Withholding them is simply inhumane.

Opioids Are Not an Effective Solution for Chronic Pain

"Painkillers don't kill pain. They kill people."

—Dr. Don Teater, medical adviser to the National Safety Council

Quoted in Elaine Silvestrini, "Profiting from Pain," Drugwatch, December 15, 2017. www.drugwatch.com.

Consider these questions as you read:

1. Taking into account the facts and ideas presented in this discussion, how persuasive is the argument that opioids are not an effective treatment for chronic pain? Which reasons are strongest and why?
2. Do you think that prescribing increasingly high doses of opioids is ever justified as a means to control chronic pain? Why or why not?
3. Do you agree with the theory that opioid-induced hyperalgesia is a natural response to painkillers? Why or why not?

Editor's note: The discussion that follows presents common arguments made in support of this perspective, reinforced by facts, quotes, and examples taken from various sources.

In the late 1990s doctors began prescribing opioids for all types of chronic pain. Dentists would give patients a thirty-day supply of opioids for routine dental procedures; people with chronic conditions such as back pain or arthritis would be placed on opioids permanently; and children with minor sports injuries would be prescribed opioids by their team doctor. In fact, opioid prescribing was so common that injured high school football players would be given opioids before games. One such player was Carter, who played high school football and baseball in a wealthy suburb in California. "With no break from sports during the year, he battled injuries that never healed," explains Sam Quinones, author of *Dreamland: The True Tale of America's Opiate Epidemic*. "A doctor prescribed Vicodin for him, with no warning on what Vicodin contained or suggestions for

19

how it should be used."[21] Carter eventually became addicted to painkillers and later to heroin.

Doctors now understand that opioids are not the best treatment for most types of chronic pain. In fact, opioids can actually increase pain in some patients and reduce their quality of life. In addition, those who do experience relief from opioids tend to be people with risk factors for addiction. For this reason, most experts agree with the CDC's 2016 official guidelines for opioid prescribing, which state that opioids should not be the first line of treatment for chronic pain.

Opioids Are Not Effective for Chronic Pain

"Chronic pain is not treated well with opiates," explains Dr. Jane Ballantyne, a pain specialist who teaches anesthesiology and pain medicine at the University of Washington. "There are a lot of common pain conditions, particularly back pain, and all the central pain syndromes—including fibromyalgia, irritable bowel syndrome, pelvic pain syndromes, and headaches . . . do badly when treated with opiates."[22] Most pain specialists agree, in part because they see in their own patients that opioids are not working. According to Dr. Muhammad Farhan, medical director of the University of Missouri pain management program, "Most of the time what I see is that [pain patients] are taking high doses of opioids and that they are in bed all the time, or sleeping and still in pain."[23]

> "Chronic pain is not treated well with opiates."[22]
>
> —Dr. Jane Ballantyne, pain specialist and anesthesiology professor

One reason that opioids do not work well to treat chronic pain is because of tolerance. Because the body compensates when pain is suppressed, opioids taken for chronic pain are only effective for a short time. Tolerance causes pain to return more quickly, which means that pain patients need to take their medicine more frequently, at higher and higher dosages. This can quickly spiral out of control and lead to addiction.

Another reason opioids are a bad choice for chronic pain patients is a phenomenon known as opioid-induced hyperalgesia, a condition that makes some opioid users more sensitive to pain. One scientist to study this phenomenon in opioid users was Mark Hutchinson, a graduate student in Australia in the late 1990s. He tested the pain response of patients who were being treated with methadone (an opioid used to ease the withdrawal symptoms of recovering heroin addicts) by submerging their forearms in ice water. Healthy control patients managed to stand the cold water for about a minute, but opioid addicts averaged only fifteen seconds. "These aren't wimps," Hutchinson said. "These people are injecting all sorts of crazy crap into their arms. . . . But they were finding this excruciating."[24] Even though the patients were currently taking opioids, they were more sensitive to pain than people who had never been addicted to opioids.

> "Your body fights back and says, 'I'm blindfolded to pain by all these chemicals. I need to be able to sense pain again.'"[25]
>
> —Pain specialist Dr. Martin Angst

Scientists do not completely understand the phenomenon of opioid-induced hyperalgesia. According to anesthesiologist Martin Angst, hyperalgesia may simply be a natural response to high doses of painkillers. "Nature didn't come up with pain just to torture mankind," he explains. Pain is central to survival, alerting the body that it is being harmed. However, when pain receptors are blocked for long periods by opioids, Angst explains, "your body fights back and says, "'I'm blindfolded to pain by all these chemicals. I need to be able to sense pain again.'"[25] Angst and other experts believe that the brain increases pain sensitivity to compensate. When opioids are withdrawn, mild levels of pain can feel excruciating. Researchers now suspect that hyperalgesia is why pain patients do not do well on opioids—the pain-blocking effects of the drug actually make their pain worse.

Patients Who Use Opioids Have Bad Outcomes

Some pain patients claim that they rely on their opioids to function—to manage their pain enough so that they can return to work or be able to take care of their children. However, scientists are beginning to

Doctors Say Opioids Are Not the Best Treatment for Chronic Pain

In 2017 the Pain News Network asked doctors whether opioids were the best treatment for patients suffering from chronic pain. Of the two hundred doctors who responded, about two-thirds agreed that there were better and safer treatments than opioids. This strongly supports the idea that opioids should not be used to treat patients who suffer from chronic pain.

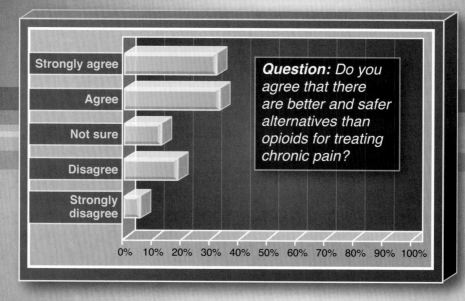

Question: Do you agree that there are better and safer alternatives than opioids for treating chronic pain?

Source: Pain News Network, "2017 CDC Survey Results," 2018. www.painnewsnetwork.org.

understand that opioids can actually reduce functioning. According to psychologist Murray McAllister, "Long-term use of opioids is associated with increasing disability, not reducing disability."[26]

While research in this area is scant, McAllister cites six scientific studies that show that opioid use correlates with chronic absence from work, more days on work-related disability, and unemployment. A 2013 study reported in the medical journal *Pain* followed 715 patients with back pain and found that those who were treated with opioids reported slightly worse functioning after six months of treatment than those who were treated with nonopioid medication. McAllister also notes that studies show that patients treated with opioids in the long term are more likely to visit the emergency room for their pain. Thus, the belief that pain patients must have opioids to function appears to be false. In fact, the opposite appears to be true.

Perhaps the most disturbing finding in regard to opioid use among chronic pain patients is that the patients who report success with opioids tend to have risk factors for addiction. As McAllister explains, "Numerous studies consistently show that patients who remain on long-term opioid management are those who, on average, have significantly higher rates of mental health and substance abuse problems."[27] Researchers are not sure why this is so, but it may be because these patients have underlying issues (which may be biological, psychological, or both) that make it more difficult for them to experience pleasure or satisfaction. This, in turn, might make them more susceptible to mental illness and more impacted by the euphoria associated with illicit substances.

> "Long-term use of opioids is associated with increasing disability, not reducing disability."[26]
>
> —Psychologist Murray McAllister

McAllister notes that this finding should not be a surprise. He writes, "If we, as healthcare providers, were honest with ourselves, we would have to admit that it is commonplace to see . . . chronic pain patients who, because of their psychological vulnerabilities, simply lose control of their use of opioids and become addicted. And we see it too often."[28] This is yet another reason why doctors must stop prescribing opioids to patients with chronic pain—even if they insist that they need the medication. Those patients who insist the loudest may also be the patients most likely to become addicted to opioids.

Opioids Are No Better than Other Painkillers

Because of these poor outcomes, some doctors have suspected that opioids may be no more effective than other types of pain medicines for chronic pain. This was confirmed in a groundbreaking 2018 study published in the *Journal of the American Medical Association*. The study included 240 patients who suffered from back pain or arthritis pain in their joints. Half were treated with opioids and half were treated with nonopioid painkillers. One year later, the two groups seemed to fare the same. "There was really no difference between the groups in terms of pain interference with activities," said Dr. Erin Krebs, lead author of the study. "And over time, the nonopioid group had less pain intensity and the opioid group had more side effects."[29] Side effects included constipation, fatigue, and nausea. This study confirms that, for back pain and arthritis pain, opioids offer no advantage over nonopioid treatments and may actually be less effective when taken over long periods.

Evidence is mounting that the medical profession has made a grave error in irresponsibly prescribing opioids for so many years. Opioids are not an effective treatment for chronic pain; in fact, they seem to make things worse. Therefore, it is imperative that the medical community develop a safe, effective, and nonaddictive treatment for chronic pain.

Chapter Two

Who Is Responsible for the Opioid Epidemic?

The Pharmaceutical Industry Created the Opioid Epidemic

- Big Pharma falsely claimed that opioids are not addictive to pain patients.
- Purdue Pharma misled doctors by claiming that high-dosage, time-release opioids are less addictive than faster-acting formulations.
- Purdue Pharma promoted the concept of pseudoaddiction with virtually no scientific proof.
- Big Pharma used deceptive marketing practices and incentives to persuade doctors to prescribe opioids for chronic pain.

The Debate at a Glance

The Pharmaceutical Industry Did Not Create the Opioid Epidemic

- The medical profession created a huge demand for opioids by declaring pain a condition that should be treated.
- Big Pharma acted both ethically and legally by creating drugs to meet the demand for chronic pain treatment.
- Doctors created financial incentives to overprescribe opioids to their patients.
- Failures of government agencies, such as the Drug Enforcement Administration (DEA) and the US Department of Veterans Affairs (VA), exacerbated the opioid epidemic.

The Pharmaceutical Industry Created the Opioid Epidemic

"The pharmaceutical industry is solely driven by its desire to make profits and boost its bottom line."

—Dr. Michael Carome, director of health research for the consumer group Public Citizen

Quoted in David Heath, "Drugmaker Set to Profit from an Opioid It Said Was Unsafe," CNN, October 30, 2017. www.cnn.com.

Consider these questions as you read:

1. Evaluate Big Pharma's argument that opioids are not addictive if taken as prescribed.
2. Which of Purdue Pharma's marketing strategies were deceptive, and how was that unethical?
3. How could Purdue Pharma have changed its marketing campaign and prevented the overprescription of opioids?

Editor's note: The discussion that follows presents common arguments made in support of this perspective, reinforced by facts, quotes, and examples taken from various sources.

The opioid epidemic was caused by the fraudulent claims and unethical behavior of major pharmaceutical companies—otherwise known as Big Pharma. These companies deliberately misled doctors about the addictive nature of opioids in order to make a profit. They achieved this with a threefold approach. First, they attacked the well-established fact that opioids are addictive. Second, they misled doctors about the addictive properties of high-dosage, time-release formulas, falsely claiming that they are not addictive. And third, they spread this message through unethical marketing practices.

The company that started it all was Purdue Pharma, the manufacturer of OxyContin. Because of Purdue's misleading marketing and outright deception, OxyContin became wildly popular and by 2001 had become the most frequently prescribed brand name opioid in the United States. Other pharmaceutical companies followed Purdue's lead, and soon doctors were prescribing opioids for everything from dental pain to arthritis to minor sports injuries. By the time this misleading practice was revealed, the United States had been flooded with highly addictive painkillers, and the opioid epidemic was under way.

False Claims About the Addictive Nature of Opioids

The opium poppy plant has been used for thousands of years to treat pain. Highly addictive opioids like heroin and morphine were widely used in the United States until 1915, when Congress banned heroin and began regulating the contents of drugs. Doctors became so concerned about their patients getting addicted to opioids that they reserved them almost exclusively for cancer patients and end-of-life care. They almost never prescribed opioids for chronic pain.

Purdue Pharma decided to change this. In 1996 the company introduced OxyContin, a time-release formulation of a common opioid called oxycodone. Because the oxycodone was released over a period of twelve hours, Purdue claimed it could make OxyContin extremely strong without causing pain patients to get a "high" feeling that could trigger addiction. This, Purdue said, made OxyContin both safe and nonaddictive—and therefore perfect for treating chronic pain.

First, however, Purdue had to convince primary care physicians (who typically have no specialized knowledge about addiction) that their fears about their patients getting hooked on opioid-based drugs were unfounded. To accomplish this, the company began promoting the message that when opioids are used to treat pain, addiction risk is extremely small. Pain, Purdue claimed, interrupted the addiction process and counteracted the sensation of being high. It based this claim on two studies that found almost no iatrogenic addiction (addiction that occurs even when patients take opioids in the way their doctor has prescribed) in pain patients who were prescribed opioids. According to Dr. Art Van Zee, Purdue "trained its sales representatives to carry the message that the risk of addiction [to OxyContin] was 'less than one percent'"[30] and

Big Pharma Profits from a Problem It Created

Big Pharma not only had a huge financial incentive to sell addictive opioids, they also profit from the current epidemic. According to the *Washington Post*, pharmaceutical companies make billions of dollars both from opioids and from drugs used to fight opioid abuse. US sales of opioid painkillers amounted to $9.57 billion in 2015 while combined sales of drugs that treat addiction, overdoses, and side effects range from $4.6 billion to $7.5 billion. This multi-billion dollar industry of addiction and death was created and is sustained by Big Pharma.

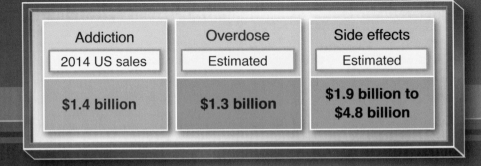

Drugs That Treat:

Addiction	Overdose	Side effects
2014 US sales	Estimated	Estimated
$1.4 billion	$1.3 billion	$1.9 billion to $4.8 billion

Source: Ariana Eunjung Cha, "The Drug Industry's Answer to Opioid Addiction: More Pills," *Washington Post*, October 16, 2016. www.washingtonpost.com.

to use these two studies to support their claims. However, these claims were wildly overblown. Both studies were of patients with acute pain, and both tracked those patients for only a short time. On the other hand, there were numerous studies available showing that up to 50 percent of chronic pain patients did develop addiction to opioids. Purdue ignored these studies.

Purdue also promoted the concept of pseudoaddiction. *Pseudoaddiction* is a term coined in 1989 by Dr. J. David Haddox, who claimed that pain patients sometimes behaved like addicts even though they were not—hoarding drugs, seeking early refills, or taking a higher dosage than prescribed. Haddox said that these patients were simply undermedicated and that their behavior would change if they got the proper dose of painkiller. In other words, if pain patients were showing signs of addiction, it just meant that they needed more of the drug. According to John Temple, author of *American Pain*, this "counterintuitive concept was based on a case study of a single cancer patient, and it hadn't been backed up by rigorous studies. Nevertheless, Purdue seized upon the new word—pseudoaddiction—and liberally sprinkled it throughout [its] educational materials."[31] The company's message was simple: Opioids are not dangerous or addictive, as long as they are taken as prescribed.

Extended-Release Opioids Cause Addiction

Purdue also needed to distinguish OxyContin from other prescription opioids on the market. It did so by claiming that OxyContin is not addictive because it is released slowly in the body over twelve hours. The problem was that OxyContin's effects do not last for twelve hours, and Purdue knew it.

An investigative report by the *Los Angeles Times* found that Purdue's own studies—bolstered by countless reports from providers and patients—revealed that many patients would experience powerful withdrawal symptoms about eight hours after taking OxyContin. According to neuropharmacologist Theodore Cicero, trying to take OxyContin every twelve hours could be "the perfect recipe for addiction." After eight hours, patients would experience a return of their pain and "the beginning stages of acute withdrawal," says Cicero. "That becomes a very powerful motivator for people to take more drugs."[32] Elizabeth Kipp experienced these acute withdrawal symptoms. After eight hours, Kipp says, "I was watching the clock. . . . My whole nervous system is on red alert." She says that for a year and a half, she cycled through misery and relief each day, which she called "a description of hell."[33]

> "I was watching the clock. . . . My whole nervous system is on red alert. . . . [It was] a description of hell."[33]
>
> —Elizabeth Kipp, who suffered daily withdrawal symptoms from OxyContin

Rather than recommend that OxyContin be taken at eight-hour intervals, Purdue simply told doctors to prescribe patients who complained of withdrawal symptoms higher and higher doses of the drug—even though higher doses of opioids increased the chance of abuse, addiction, and overdose. An example of one victim of this practice was police officer Ernest Gallego, who was prescribed OxyContin for a back injury. "He was having car accidents, fender benders. Very groggy all the time. He spent much of his day sleeping,"[34] Gallego's sister says. Gallego later died of an overdose of the high-potency pills he had been prescribed, which he had been abusing to manage his pain.

> "The Q12 [every twelve hours] dosing schedule [of OxyContin] is an addiction producing machine."[37]
>
> —Dr. David Egilman

As reports of OxyContin addiction accumulated, Purdue continued to instruct its sales force to mislead doctors about the addictive nature of the drug. One sales manager told a state investigator that his superiors "told us to say things like it is 'virtually' non-addicting."[35] The reason, as revealed by Purdue's lawyers, was to maximize profit. "The 12 hour dosing schedule represents a significant competitive advantage of OxyContin over other products,"[36] the lawyers wrote in a court document.

The Public Fights Back

As the opioid crisis grew, the public began to fight back against Purdue's deceptive practices. In 2002 Purdue was sued for overstating the duration of the effectiveness of OxyContin. The night before trial, Purdue settled the case: In exchange for contributing $10 million to state drug abuse programs, Purdue would not have to admit wrongdoing or change the way it told doctors to prescribe the drug. More lawsuits followed. In 2007 three of Purdue's executives pled guilty to misleading doctors about the addictive nature of OxyContin and were fined a total of $634.5 million. Purdue Pharma itself was not impacted by the ruling, and it continued to recommend twelve-hour dosing. In 2008 Dr. David Egilman, an expert on warning labels, told the US Food and Drug Administration (FDA) that "the Q12 [every twelve hours] dosing schedule is an addiction producing machine."[37] The FDA did not respond. OxyContin sales continued to grow. In 2014 doctors wrote 5.4 million prescriptions for the drug.

Purdue has been sued thousands of times since it released OxyContin, but OxyContin is not the only dangerous opioid on the market. Major pharmaceutical companies like Johnson & Johnson, Pfizer, and Endo Pharmaceuticals have their own versions of opioid-based painkillers and have been similarly accused of deliberately deceiving doctors about their potential for abuse. By 2018 there were hundreds of lawsuits against these companies, many brought by state governments, who claim that Big Pharma is responsible for the massive costs associated with the scourge of opioid addiction that has overwhelmed their communities. In response to the growing outcry against Big Pharma, the FDA has increased warnings on opioid packaging. But as of 2018, the FDA still had not banned these dangerous drugs.

By misleading doctors about opioids being safe and nonaddictive, Big Pharma caused the opioid crisis. The industry charged with bringing new, lifesaving drugs to the public has spawned an epidemic that kills tens of thousands of people each year. Big Pharma has acted fraudulently and unethically again and again, and without legal checks, it will continue its deceptive practices. Big Pharma must be held accountable for the damage it has done and continues to do.

The Pharmaceutical Industry Did Not Create the Opioid Epidemic

"Let's be realistic about this: a prescription can only be filled if a doctor writes it. So when people say, how did this all begin? How did this all start? It started because a prescription was written."

—Mike Fasano, former Florida legislator

Quoted in Nick Evans, "Why Isn't It Mandatory for Doctors to Use a State Drug Monitoring Database?," WFSU News, November 3, 2017. http://news.wfsu.org.

Consider these questions as you read:

1. Taking into account the facts and ideas presented in this discussion, do you agree that doctors, not Big Pharma, created the opioid epidemic? Explain your answer, citing from the text.
2. Do you think that pharmaceutical distributors should have refused to fill suspicious opioid orders, or was alerting the DEA enough? Why or why not?
3. What role has the government, including the DEA and the VA, played in the opioid epidemic? Use examples from the text in your answer.

Editor's note: The discussion that follows presents common arguments made in support of this perspective, reinforced by facts, quotes, and examples taken from various sources.

The media has promoted a narrative that major pharmaceutical companies—often referred to as Big Pharma—caused the opioid crisis. The story goes that Big Pharma somehow persuaded doctors to overprescribe opioids for chronic pain, flooding the United States with prescription painkillers that were then diverted for recreational use. The truth is that doctors overprescribed for a variety of reasons, but none of those involved the pharmaceutical industry. Doctors, not pharmaceutical companies, created a huge demand for opioids in their pain patients and then asked Big Pharma to meet this demand.

Big Pharma Did Not Create Opioid Demand

The medical profession, not Big Pharma, created a huge demand for opioids as a treatment for chronic pain. In the 1970s and 1980s, doctors rarely prescribed opioids for pain, causing the unnecessary suffering of thousands of people with intractable pain. In response to this, in the 1990s there was a movement among those in the medical profession to regard pain as an unnatural state that they were ethically obligated to remedy. The American Pain Society named pain as the fifth vital sign, along with blood pressure, heart rate, respiratory rate, and temperature. Making pain one of the vital signs meant that doctors were ethically responsible for addressing it—which meant reducing or eliminating it.

Respected physicians like pain specialist Russell Portenoy began advocating opioid use to treat intractable pain; Portenoy described opioids as a "gift from nature"[38] in 1993. Some states passed legislation that codified this idea; for instance, California created a Pain Patient's Bill of Rights in 1996, which

> "We changed our prescription pads to allow and accommodate for stronger prescriptions overnight."[40]
>
> —Dr. Roneet Lev, chair of the Prescription Drug Abuse Medical Task Force

in a 2001 revision stated that a chronic pain patient "should have access to proper treatment of his or her pain" and that "opiates administered for severe acute and severe chronic intractable pain can be safe."[39] Very quickly, the medical profession as a whole began prioritizing the reduction of intractable pain. According to Dr. Roneet Lev, chair of the Prescription Drug Abuse Medical Task Force, "We changed our prescription pads to allow and accommodate for stronger prescriptions overnight."[40]

It was this shift in attitude that created a demand for opioids. Companies like Purdue Pharma—a for-profit business in a highly regulated industry—simply created new formulations of opioids to meet this demand.

Hillside Public Library

Big Pharma Does Not Regulate Opioid Distribution

The pharmaceutical industry has also been accused of distributing Oxy-Contin and other opioid formulations in high numbers to certain pain clinics and pharmacies that were overprescribing or selling drugs illicitly. However, it is not Big Pharma's role to deny doctors the medication they legally prescribe. This is the job of the government, which sets limits on how many pills can be produced each year and tracks who buys opioids and in what quantities. According to John Gray, president and chief executive officer of the pharmaceutical distributing company Healthcare Distribution Alliance, "Expecting distributors to have unilaterally stemmed the flow of opioids—a flow that increased yearly with the explicit oversight and approval of the DEA—is a transparent attempt by former DEA officials to shift the blame for their own failed approach to regulation during the growth and peak of the epidemic."[41]

John Hammergren, chief executive of the pharmaceutical distributor McKesson Corporation, believes that the DEA should have investigated suspicious orders more quickly. "If the pharmacies filling prescriptions or the doctors writing prescriptions were known by the DEA to be 'rogue' at the time," he says, "why the DEA allowed them to keep their registrations and failed to share its suspicions with us is a mystery."[42] The truth is that these orders for opioids were both legal and monitored by the DEA, and it is the DEA, not Big Pharma, that is responsible for investigating suspicious orders.

Doctors Incentivized to Prescribe Opioids

Doctors had strong financial incentives to overprescribe opioids in the 1990s—but they were incentives created by the practices of their own profession. When the medical profession established pain as the fifth vital sign, it began educating patients about their right to pain relief. Doctors were trained to accept at face value a patient's interpretation of their level of pain, and many exam rooms posted notices that explained that patients had a right to request relief of this pain. As addiction specialist Dr. Glenn Simon explains, "Categorizing pain as the fifth vital sign conditioned patients to expect that providers would 'normalize' it in

Irresponsible Prescribing Continues to Fuel Opioid Epidemic

Although opioid prescribing is on the decline, a 2018 report revealed that there were still about six times as many opioid prescriptions filled in the United States in 2017 than there were in 1992. This is the equivalent of fifty-two pills per adult per year dispensed in 2017, as compared to twenty-two pills in 1992. This suggests that doctors were not only the cause of the opioid epidemic but that they continue to fuel it with irresponsible prescribing practices.

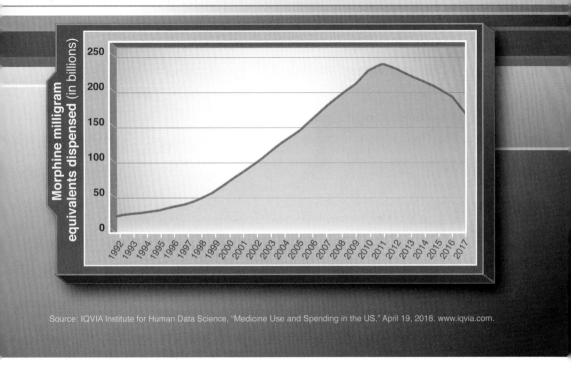

Source: IQVIA Institute for Human Data Science, "Medicine Use and Spending in the US," April 19, 2018. www.iqvia.com.

the same way that they normalize the other four vital signs."[43] In other words, patients received the message that they had a right to be pain free. Since opioids were the preferred treatment for pain, patients came to expect an opioid prescription. And when they did not receive one, they often thought their doctors were not doing their jobs.

At the same time, the medical profession began including pain relief in its satisfaction surveys. As journalist Christopher Caldwell explains, "'Chronic pain' became a condition, not just a symptom. . . . Patients threatened malpractice suits against doctors who did not prescribe pain medications liberally, and gave them bad marks on the 'patient satisfaction' surveys that, in some insurance programs, determine doctor compensation."[44] Patient satisfaction surveys are also a significant factor in a hospital's ranking. In addition, in the digital age many people choose their doctors on the basis of their ranking in an online review site. In other words, by creating an expectation for pain relief and tying their own compensation to patient satisfaction, doctors inadvertently created a huge incentive to keep their patients happy. Too often, this meant writing them a prescription for opioids.

Doctors Irresponsibly Overprescribed Opioids

Finally, doctors overprescribed opioids due to their own irresponsible practices. The health care industry has created a situation in which family doctors spend about fifteen minutes with each patient. As Simon explains, "Today, employed doctors are paid based on the number of patients they see in a day. . . . A patient's time spent with their doctor has become as much about meeting production quotas as about patient care."[45] Addiction specialist Dr. Anna Lembke calls this "the Toyotazation of medicine"[46]—a process in which patients move through practices like cars on an assembly line. Family practitioners had no time to screen patients for addiction issues or do their own research about opioid addiction. They simply gave their patients what they asked for.

Perhaps the most shocking example of irresponsible prescribing practices involves Veterans Affairs Medical Centers (VAMCs), hospitals throughout the country that treat veterans of the US armed forces. According to journalist Art Levine, author of the book *Mental Health, Inc.*, "The Department of Veterans Affairs has played a little-discussed role in fueling the opioid epidemic that is killing civilians and veterans alike. In 2011, veterans were twice as likely to die from accidental opioid overdoses as non-veterans."[47] Levine explains that from 2001 to 2013, opioid prescribing at VAMCs increased by 500 percent, while the patient load increased by less than 40 percent.

A glaring example of this problem can be found in a 2015 statement by the VAMC in Huntington, West Virginia, which stated it was prescribing about 18 percent of its patients opioids in 2012—a rate that is 230 percent higher than the national average. Many of these prescriptions went to patients who were not properly examined or who had pain with no physical cause. Noelle Johnson, a VAMC pharmacist, was fired after she refused to fill a thirty-day supply of 1,080 morphine pills to treat a patient's "psychological pain." And a VAMC doctor who asked to remain anonymous said to CBS News, "I have seen people that have not had an exam of that body part that they're complaining of pain in for two years. It's easier to write a prescription for [opioids], and just move along, get to the next patient."[48]

> "It's easier to write a prescription for [opioids], and just move along, get to the next patient."[48]
>
> —VAMC doctor

The pharmaceutical industry is not responsible for the opioid epidemic. It simply did what it was designed to do—meet the needs of the medical profession. Doctors created the expectation in their patients that pain relief was a right. They tied their compensation to patient satisfaction, and they prescribed opioids irresponsibly. It was this "perfect storm" of factors that flooded the United States with opioids and led to the current crisis—not the behavior of Big Pharma.

Chapter Three

Can Regulating Opioid Prescriptions More Strictly Prevent Their Abuse?

Regulating Opioid Prescriptions More Strictly Will Help Prevent Abuse

- Regulations that put limits on opioid prescriptions are necessary to stop overprescribing.
- The most effective way to stop "doctor shopping" and to hold doctors accountable for their prescribing practices is to mandate that all doctors use prescription drug monitoring programs (PDMPs).
- Mandated education can ensure that doctors who prescribe opioids will properly screen for addiction.

The Debate at a Glance

Regulating Opioid Prescriptions More Strictly Will Encourage Abuse

- PDMPs encourage doctors to drop pain patients who genuinely need opioids.
- Regulations place unfair burdens on pain patients, such as forcing them to travel hundreds of miles to renew a prescription.
- Pain patients who face these barriers are more likely to buy pain pills on the black market, which can lead to addiction.

Regulating Opioid Prescriptions More Strictly Will Help Prevent Abuse

"The [PDMP] systems that are mandatory are the ones that are having an impact and saving people's lives."

—Ricardo Lara, California state senator

Quoted in Lenny Bernstein, "New State Rules Are Forcing Opioid Prescribers to Confront 'Doctor Shopping,'" *Washington Post*, January 14, 2017. www.washingtonpost.com.

Consider these questions as you read:

1. How persuasive is the argument that all doctors should be forced to use their state's PDMP? Explain.
2. The state of New Jersey limits all first-time painkiller prescriptions to five days. Do you agree with this law, or would you change it? Explain your reasoning.
3. Do you think regulations are the best way to stop doctors from prescribing so many opioids? Why or why not?

Editor's note: The discussion that follows presents common arguments made in support of this perspective, reinforced by facts, quotes, and examples taken from various sources.

The current opioid epidemic in the United States can be traced back to the late 1990s and early 2000s, when doctors overprescribed opioid pain medication. In some cases, doctors did not understand the drugs' potential for abuse; in others, doctors behaved unethically, operating what have come to be known as pill mills—pain clinics that routinely prescribe opioids to addicted patients for nonmedical reasons. Despite an increase in regulations designed to shut down pill mills and curb overprescribing, opioids are still being overprescribed, and people are continuing to be led down the path of addiction, overdose, and death. Only by strengthening regulations that curtail overprescribing can this epidemic be stopped.

A Seven-Day Prescription Is Enough

Beginning in the 1990s doctors began to use opioids to treat any type of pain, including pain related to sports injuries, dental procedures, backaches, arthritis, and even occasional headaches. It also was—and in some places, still is—common practice for doctors to prescribe a month's worth of prescription painkillers at a time, regardless of how long a patient was expected to experience pain. For instance, in 2015 Ross White was issued a prescription for thirty Percocet tablets by an emergency room in Virginia that treated him for kidney stone pain—even though he left the hospital pain free. "I certainly didn't need thirty pills," White said. "Did they expect me to have thirty more kidney stone attacks before I saw my doctor?" Like many people, Ross kept the excess pills, not realizing that opioids are often diverted (meaning transferred to another person for illicit use). "They're gone now," he said. "I think my nephew stole them. It makes me sick to think about it."[49]

Diversion is not the only problem related to overprescribing. Research has shown that the longer a person takes opioids, the greater the chance he or she will become addicted to them. "Even at relatively low doses and low duration of opioid use, the risk of long-term use and dependency begins to escalate very early on," explains Dr. Richard Deyo, who teaches public health and preventative medicine at Oregon Health and Science University. "It's time to begin prescribing opioids for fewer patients, for fewer days and for smaller doses than we have in the past."[50] In 2016 the CDC issued opioid prescribing guidelines that recommended that doctors prescribe "no greater quantity than needed for the expected duration of pain severe

> "It's time to begin prescribing opioids for fewer patients, for fewer days and for smaller doses than we have in the past."[50]
>
> —Dr. Richard Deyo

enough to require opioids. Three days or less will often be sufficient; more than seven days will rarely be needed."[51]

As of April 2017, thirteen states had responded to the guidance by limiting most opioid prescriptions to seven days. New Jersey, which has one of the strictest laws in the country, limits all opioid prescriptions to five days. However, too many states still do not limit first-time opioid prescribing to less than thirty days. In addition, a recent report from the CDC that looked at prescribing trends found that the average length of opioid prescriptions increased from thirteen days in

> "The bottom line is that too many [people] are still getting too much for too long."[52]
>
> —CDC principal deputy director Anne Schuchat

2006 to eighteen days in 2015. And despite a slight decrease in overall prescribing, the CDC found that doctors are still prescribing more than three times the number of opioids as they did in 1999. "The bottom line is that too many [people] are still getting too much for too long,"[52] says CDC principal deputy director Anne Schuchat.

Clearly, current regulations are not doing enough to curb opioid prescribing. Unilateral regulations need to be imposed on all states to limit opioid prescriptions, both to reduce incidences of accidental addiction and to limit access to these powerful drugs, which are too often diverted and misused.

Track Opioid Prescribing

One of the most effective tools in the effort to reduce opioid prescriptions is PDMPs. These are state-run electronic databases that monitor doctors' prescribing histories to make sure they comply with their state's regulations. According to Meghna Patel, director of Pennsylvania's PDMP program, research has shown that requiring the use of PDMPs "significantly helps in cutting down overprescribing patterns, which then cuts down on opioid overdoses."[53]

PDMPs first came into use in 2010. The CDC reports that by 2015 half of all counties in the United States experienced a 17 percent reduction

Regulations Stop "Doctor Shopping"

When New York doctors were forced to check the state's Prescription Drug Monitoring Program (PDMP) database when prescribing opioids, incidences of patients successfully getting multiple prescriptions filled, or "doctor shopping," were nearly eliminated. This is why all states should pass regulations that make PDMP use mandatory for opioid prescribers.

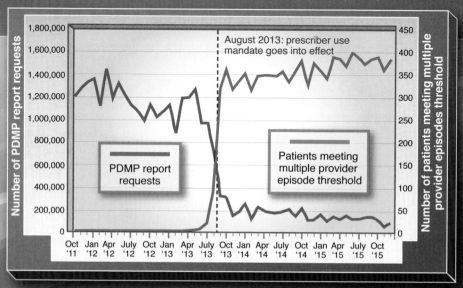

Note: Multiple provider episodes defined as patients using five or more prescribers and five or more dispensers within the month.

Source: Pew Charitable Trusts, *Prescription Drug Monitoring Programs*, December 2016. www.pewtrusts.org.

in opioid prescribing, on average. In states that mandate PDMP use, the reduction can be dramatic. For instance, two states with mandated PDMP use, Ohio and Kentucky, found that opioid prescribing declined in 85 percent and 62 percent of their counties, respectively. According to the CDC, these findings indicate that "substantial changes [in opioid prescribing] are possible" and these changes "can save lives."[54]

As of 2018 every state in the nation had its own PDMP, and some share information across state lines. However, eleven states still do not have laws that require doctors to use their PDMPs. According to the

Trump administration, when PDMP use is not required, only about 35 percent of physicians participate; but when it is mandatory, a whopping 90 percent participate. For this reason, Congress needs to pass the Prescription Drug Monitoring Act. This act would mandate the use of PDMPs by all doctors in states that receive funding to fight the opioid epidemic. It would also require doctors to use their PDMPs within twenty-four hours of dispensing a controlled substance, so that patients who are doctor shopping (a term that means seeing multiple doctors for the same complaint in order to get multiple prescriptions) can be identified. This would not only help doctors identify patients who are misusing opioids and may be addicted, it will also force doctors to be accountable to their licensing board if they are overprescribing opioids.

Mandated Education Is Key

While regulations that limit opioid prescriptions and require doctors to participate in PDMPs are key components of the fight against opioid addiction, they will not be effective unless all doctors who prescribe opioids are trained in addressing addiction issues. If they are not, they will be more inclined to simply refuse to treat their pain patients. According to anesthesiologist Jane Ballantyne, "When you introduce laws and regulations, you can produce a situation where physicians are less inclined to prescribe, or are even frightened of prescribing, because when it becomes a law, it is an issue of their medical license and therefore their livelihood. That can be quite a potent factor in discouraging people from prescribing."[55] Pain patients—especially those who may be dependent on high levels of opioids—cannot simply stop taking these drugs without enduring unacceptable levels of suffering, and those who are dropped by their doctors are more likely to seek relief from their pain from illicit sources like the black market, where medications are unregulated and sometimes contain deadly levels of opioids.

For this reason, Congress should pass the Safer Prescribing of Controlled Substances Act. This act would require opioid prescribers to undergo mandatory training on safe prescribing practices, as well as training on how to identify those patients who may have a substance use disorder or be at risk of developing one. "Most substance abuse disorders start with a prescription pad," says Senator Richard Blumenthal, a cosponsor of the act. "With our country awash in opioids there is an urgent need to ensure that the gatekeepers to these drugs are trained in responsible practices and given the tools they need to spot potential abuse before it happens."[56]

Stricter regulations and PDMPs represent the best tools available to reverse the opioid addiction epidemic and stop new cases of addiction. However, if these regulations are to be effective, they must be paired with a mandated education program for opioid prescribers. Doctors must be enabled to help their patients with both their pain and addiction issues while practicing safe prescribing practices. Only by strengthening regulations, making PDMP participation mandatory, and providing effective education and support to doctors can the nation reverse the epidemic of opioid abuse, addiction, and overdose.

Regulating Opioid Prescriptions More Strictly Will Encourage Abuse

"If you . . . needed [opioids] badly for pain relief, what would you do if your prescription was abruptly terminated? . . . You'd try your best to get relief elsewhere. And your odds of overdosing would increase astronomically."

—Neuroscientist Marc Lewis

Marc Lewis, "The Truth About the US 'Opioid Crisis'—Prescriptions Aren't the Problem," *Guardian* (Manchester), November 7, 2017. www.theguardian.com.

Consider these questions as you read:

1. Taking into account the facts and ideas presented in this discussion, how persuasive is the argument that further regulating opioid prescriptions encourages addiction? Which reasons are strongest and why?
2. In what ways do regulations interfere with the doctor-patient relationship? Use examples from the text to support your answer.
3. Why would tracking opioid prescriptions cause doctors to drop pain patients?

Editor's note: The discussion that follows presents common arguments made in support of this perspective, reinforced by facts, quotes, and examples taken from various sources.

Marlene is a forty-two-year-old woman who has a rare blood-clotting disorder that causes intense pain in her legs. She lives in public housing in Indiana—a state with strict laws regulating opioid prescribing practices. Because of these laws, her primary care physician dropped her, claiming her pain was too complex for him to treat. By the time emergency room doctors realized that blood clots had formed in her legs and were blocking blood flow, her legs had to be amputated. After surgery, Marlene was given a prescription for only seven days' worth of opioid painkillers, as mandated by law. But because she had no primary care doctor to advocate for her, Medicaid refused to cover the prescription, and she had to pay $400 out of pocket—money that she could not afford.

Current laws regulating opioid prescribing practices are destroying the lives of people like Marlene—patients with complex conditions that cause them intense pain. These strict regulations interfere with the doctor-patient relationship, preventing doctors from using their extensive knowledge and training to properly care for their patients. Instead, regulations pressure doctors to drop pain patients and encourage insurance companies to refuse to cover prescriptions. "Rather than spending the right money for the right pain care delivered to persons with complex needs, we are focused on managing dose, counting pills, [and] rationing appointments," writes Terri Lewis, a pain specialist. She says this is resulting in the "blackballing of patients with complex care needs."[57]

Because of these strict prescribing regulations, patients who once had their pain managed effectively suddenly face insurmountable barriers to health care. And those who are cut off by their doctors may become so desperate that they buy pain pills on the black market—pills that are often laced with another powerful opioid called fentanyl. Thus, regulating prescriptions to fight opioid abuse is actually having a reverse effect—the practice is putting the very people opioids are designed to treat at risk of addiction and overdose.

Pain Patients Do Not Become Addicts

Most regulations are designed to curb opioid overprescribing. The assumption is that doctors are prescribing far too many opioids to their patients, who then become addicts. However, pain patients make up a very small percentage of people who suffer from opioid addiction. According to Dr. Jeffrey Singer, a surgeon and senior fellow at the Cato Institute, "The sequence that everybody thinks exists, in which a patient gets narcotics for pain, gets hooked, and then eventually dies from an overdose, is not your typical story."[58] Singer notes that a 2014 study published in the *Journal of the American Medical Association* found that,

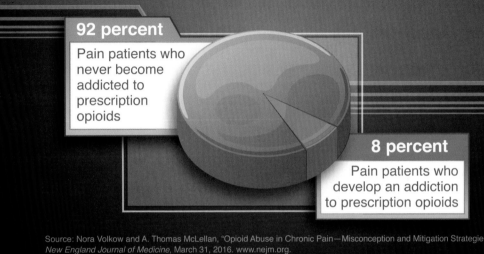

Regulations That Limit Opioid Prescriptions Are Unnecessary

Because pain patients who are prescribed opioids rarely develop opioid addiction, regulations that limit their access to opioids are unnecessary. According to published studies that distinguish addiction (craving and drug-seeking behavior) from dependency (physical withdrawal without craving), less than 8 percent of pain patients become addicted to opioids.

92 percent
Pain patients who never become addicted to prescription opioids

8 percent
Pain patients who develop an addiction to prescription opioids

Source: Nora Volkow and A. Thomas McLellan, "Opioid Abuse in Chronic Pain—Misconception and Mitigation Strategies," *New England Journal of Medicine*, March 31, 2016. www.nejm.org.

of 136,000 patients treated for overdoses, only 13 percent were chronic pain patients. In Singer's experience, patients who develop physical dependence on opioids (experiencing physical withdrawal symptoms without craving the drug) want to be weaned off their medication. They do not become addicts. However, the current strategy to fight the opioid epidemic ignores this fact. Instead of targeting the illegal use of opioids, it targets doctors who write legal prescriptions for their patients.

Tracking Opioid Prescribers Pressures Doctors to Drop Patients

The tools most commonly used to pressure doctors into writing fewer opioid prescriptions are PDMPs. These are state databases designed to flag patients who are using high doses of opioids and penalize the doctors who prescribe them. Doctors who prescribe a lot of opioids are flagged as outliers, which brings them to the attention of their state licensing board and law enforcement. For instance, Dr. Forest Tennant, one of the few physicians left in the United States willing to treat patients who live with severe, intractable pain, was raided by the DEA in November 2017 because he prescribes very high doses of opioids to a handful of his patients. According to Dr. Lynn Webster, a pain specialist who was also raided, the DEA is targeting prominent pain specialists like him and Tennant to "intimidate other doctors who prescribe opioids to pain patients."[59] Tennant agrees. "They figure if they go after the big guy," he says, "then no doctor is going to be willing to prescribe or do anything."[60]

Unfortunately, this tactic is working. Countless pain patients are being dropped by their primary care providers or pain specialists because the doctors fear being singled out as outliers in their PDMPs. "Nobody wants to be seen as an outlier," writes Singer. "It pressures doctors to cut back on prescribing, and then their legitimately suffering patients are driven to the illegal market where they get laced opioids, or they go to cheaper heroin and, of course, that is where the overdoses occur."[61]

Barriers Can Drive Patients to the Black Market

Pain patients who can find doctors to treat them still face substantial barriers to care. Most are required to be seen frequently by pain specialists, who may not be covered by the patients' insurance or may not practice in their area. Other pain patients—who once were told that they had a right to pain relief—now face suspicion and humiliation. Many are forced to submit to urine tests and addiction screenings to assure their prescribers that they are not abusing their medication. Even patients who are at the end of their lives—the very people for whom addiction should not be a consideration—are affected by the shift in attitudes

> "Is this country going to treat pain patients or not? Are they going to let people die in pain or are they not?"[63]
>
> —Dr. Forest Tennant

about opioids. Dr. Susan Glod, who provides palliative care to dying patients, states that her patients face unfair judgment and hostility for past substance abuse. One such patient was called a "monster" by a nurse who did not want to give him the pain medication Glod prescribed. Glod writes that the war on opioids "should not come at a cost to the epidemic's other victims—hospice patients . . . whose history of substance abuse, no matter how remote, determines whether their pain will be treated; patients like Jerry, who, dying from cancer, his body containing more tumor than anything else, was told he is a monster."[62]

> "Stop interfering in the patient-doctor relationship—you're actually making it worse."[65]
>
> —Dr. Jeffrey Singer

All of these barriers take a toll on patients. Many do not have the money to pay for a pain specialist out of pocket or the resources to travel great distances for care. Others have conditions that make it impossible for them to get to the frequent appointments and drug tests required in their state. And when they lose their prescriptions or cannot afford the costs associated with getting them, some inevitably turn to the black market, where the cost of heroin is a fraction that of a prescription painkiller. These patients are not addicts—they are desperate for pain relief. "I think there needs to be an outcry," says Tennant, who advocates for pain patients. "Is this country going to treat pain patients or not? Are they going to let people die in pain or are they not?"[63]

More Regulation Will Equal More Deaths

Instead of fighting the recreational opioid use that leads to addiction and overdose, the Donald Trump administration is escalating its war on doctors who prescribe opioids to pain patients. In February 2018 Attorney General Jeff Sessions announced that the US Department of Justice would be using state PDMPs to prosecute more doctors—an act that will only cause more pain patients to be dropped, driving them to buy opioids on the black market to control their pain. "If people can't get access to needed pain control meds then we will turn to street drugs that will kill us or commit suicide," writes Michelle, a pain patient who was recently dropped by her doctor. "Trust me, I've thought of both recently."[64]

The solution to the opioid abuse crisis is not to undermine the doctor-patient relationship with one-size-fits-all regulations intended to intimidate doctors and humiliate patients. Doctors are best able to determine whether their patients have a true medical need for pain relief. Regulations should be designed to encourage doctors to closely monitor their pain, not deny them pain relief. As Singer writes, "My advice [to lawmakers] would be to stop interfering in the patient-doctor relationship—you're actually making it worse."[65]

Chapter Four

Can Medical Marijuana Prevent Opioid Abuse?

Medical Marijuana Can Prevent Opioid Abuse

- Marijuana is an effective, safe, and nonaddictive painkiller that can replace opioids for chronic pain treatment.
- People with access to marijuana use fewer prescription and illicit opioids.
- Marijuana has been shown to be effective in helping opioid addicts beat their addiction.

The Debate at a Glance

Medical Marijuana Will Not Prevent Opioid Abuse

- Marijuana is harmful to developing brains, stunting the part of the brain responsible for resisting impulses and making good choices.
- Marijuana is addictive and primes the brain for addiction, especially in teens.
- Legalizing marijuana without proper study and oversight is a repeat of practices that caused the opioid epidemic.

Medical Marijuana Can Prevent Opioid Abuse

"Patients that find cannabis to be a successful treatment for their chronic pain might never have to walk down the very tricky path of opioid use."

—Philippe Lucas, medical marijuana researcher

Quoted in New Mexico State Department of Health Medical Cannabis Advisory Board, "Petition: Substance Abuse Disorder," September 27, 2017. http://lecuanmmcpmcabpetitions.blogspot.com.

Consider these questions as you read:

1. Taking into account the facts and ideas presented in this discussion, how persuasive is the argument that marijuana can prevent opioid abuse? Which reasons are strongest and why?
2. Why do you think access to marijuana reduces both prescription and illicit opioid use?
3. Do you think it is a good idea to treat opioid addicts with marijuana? Why or why not?

Editor's note: The discussion that follows presents common arguments made in support of this perspective, reinforced by facts, quotes, and examples taken from various sources.

There is no doubt that opioids are effective for some forms of acute pain. However, they are also extremely addictive—especially when taken over time for chronic conditions or for illicit, recreational purposes. For this reason scientists have been searching for a replacement for opioids—an effective painkiller that is not addictive, is not deadly in high doses, and can be taken for long periods to treat chronic conditions. Researchers often refer to such a drug as the "holy grail" of pain relief. If such a painkiller could be found, it could replace prescription opioids entirely, making them far less accessible to addicts and prevent new cases of addiction.

Medical Marijuana Reduces Opioid Use

In states where medical marijuana is legal, doctors prescribe fewer doses of painkillers for common medical conditions than in states where medical marijuana is illegal, according to a 2016 study published in the medical journal *Health Affairs*. This study corroborates a growing body of research that demonstrates that medical marijuana is an effective replacement for opioids in chronic pain patients and can substantially reduce their use.

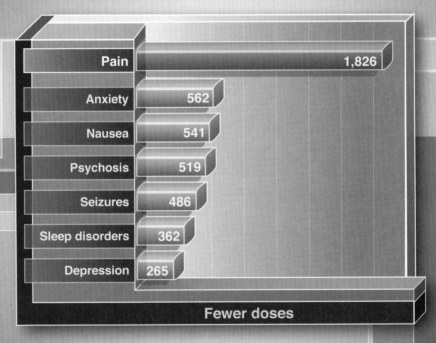

Condition	Fewer doses
Pain	1,826
Anxiety	562
Nausea	541
Psychosis	519
Seizures	486
Sleep disorders	362
Depression	265

Source: Christopher Ingraham, "One Striking Chart Shows Why Pharma Companies Are Fighting Legal Marijuana," *Washington Post*, July 13, 2016. www.washingtonpost.com.

Medical marijuana is that holy grail. Marijuana (also known as cannabis) has been used for thousands of years to treat pain, and its pain-suppressing effects are well established in medical research. Marijuana has a low potential for addiction, and any addiction-like effects that develop are largely psychological and easily treated. Marijuana is also extremely safe. According to a 2016 report by the National Cannabis Industry Association, it is "scientifically established that cannabis is far safer than any opioid, prescription or otherwise. . . . No one knows the lethal toxicity of cannabis, because there's never been a documented case of a cannabis overdose death."[66] Finally, medical marijuana is effective in helping both pain patients and addicts reduce or eliminate their dependence on opioids, helping them beat their chemical dependency or addiction.

Marijuana Is an Effective Pain Reliever

Marijuana and opioids control pain in similar ways—both occupy receptors in the brain that suppress pain and create feelings of relaxation and euphoria. However, the receptors that are occupied by marijuana affect the brain differently. They do not cause intense craving or painful withdrawal symptoms when marijuana is removed, and therefore they are not addictive. In addition, researchers have found a way to genetically manipulate the marijuana plant so that it contains high amounts of the chemical that suppresses pain but that does not maker the user high. Therefore, most strains of medical marijuana are bred so that they are highly effective in treating pain without causing the user to get high.

A wealth of recent medical research has proved that the pain-relieving chemicals in marijuana are effective in treating chronic pain. For instance, a 2015 review of scientific studies involving these chemicals found that, in 71 percent of the thirty-eight studies examined, these chemicals had "empirically demonstrable and statistically significant pain-relieving effects."[67] A 2018 report by the Minnesota Medical Cannabis Program (a state-run program that treats patients with intractable pain with medical marijuana) found that 61 percent of the program's patients reported a high level of benefit within the first five months of treatment, while only 10 percent reported little or no benefit. "I lived my life in constant pain [and] my daily pain on an average was an 8 [out of 10]," one patient said. "I started taking medical cannabis in August. I now have a daily pain average between 2 and 3."[68]

Using Marijuana Reduces Opioid Use

Using medical marijuana has also been found to reduce opioid use in pain patients—whether they have become dependent on the opioid or not. Research has found that in patients who are taking high doses of opioids, adding medical marijuana can help them reduce their dose—or even eliminate opioids altogether. For instance, Kyle Turley, a retired professional football player who had become physically dependent on opioids to treat pain caused by over one hundred concussions he suffered during his career, was able to wean himself off prescription drugs using medical marijuana. Turley explains that while opioids seemed to increase his depression, anxiety, and suicidal thoughts, marijuana had the opposite effect, effectively managing his pain without debilitating side effects. "Cannabis saved my life," he says. "I was a day away from suicide and checking out altogether. It gave me my life back, gave me my family back, and helped me get off all of the pills."[69]

Turley's experience is not uncommon. According to Dr. Dustin Sulak, who specializes in treating pain patients with medical marijuana, "Usually if a patient is taking opioids, you expect them to come back and ask for more, because their effectiveness diminishes over time. But we saw patients using cannabis decreasing and stopping their use of opioids without even being asked to. None of us had seen anything like it in any area of medicine."[70] In fact, one survey found that 78 percent of Sulak's patients either reduced (39 percent) or stopped taking (39 percent) opioids altogether.

> "I was a day away from suicide and checking out altogether. . . . [Cannabis] helped me get off all of the pills."[69]
>
> —Kyle Turley, retired professional football player

These findings are confirmed by national data about opioid prescribing. Research has shown that in states where medical marijuana is legal, doctors are prescribing fewer doses of opioids. A 2016 study of prescription drugs sold under Medicare drug sales were markedly lower in the states that had legalized medical marijuana, and the typical doctor prescribed 1,826 fewer opioids each year. "The results were very robust, particularly for pain medications," says study coauthor W. David Bradford. "This is one more piece of evidence that people are treating marijuana like medicine."[71] A follow-up study found that in 2014 medical marijuana was responsible for $178.5 million in prescription drug savings in Medicaid alone.

In addition, studies have found that in states where people have legal access to marijuana, opioid-related deaths fall. For instance, a 2014 study published in *JAMA Internal Medicine* found that states that had legalized medical marijuana reported a 25 percent decrease in opioid-related deaths. Meanwhile, a 2017 study published in the *International Journal of Drug Policy* that examined use of medical marijuana in Canada found that 30 percent of the 271 respondents said that they used marijuana as a substitute for opioids. These results imply that when people have the option of using medical marijuana for pain relief, they are more likely to choose it over opioids.

> "We saw patients using cannabis decreasing and stopping their use of opioids without even being asked to."[70]
>
> —Dr. Dustin Sulak, addiction specialist

In fact, even some recreational drug users seem to choose marijuana over opioids when marijuana is legal. According to authors of a 2017 study of opioid deaths in Colorado, "After Colorado's legalization of recreational cannabis sale and use, opioid-related deaths decreased more than 6 percent in the following 2 years."[72] These studies provide strong evidence that legal access to marijuana substantially reduces opioid prescribing, abuse, and overdose.

Marijuana Can Help People Beat Opioid Addiction

Not only can medical marijuana be used to effectively treat patients suffering from chronic pain, there is growing evidence that it can help treat the millions of people who are addicted to opioids. At High Sobriety, an addiction center in Los Angeles, California, patients use marijuana to help them tolerate opioid withdrawal symptoms and maintain their sobriety. The center's founders use marijuana to help clients sleep, develop an appetite, and recapture a sense of emotional control. According to Amanda Reiman, a consultant at the center, "There is no scientific reason to believe that somebody is better off being completely miserable and sober than using cannabis occasionally, or even fairly regularly, as an adult and being functional and happy and productive."[73]

Many pain and addiction specialists agree with this point of view and integrate marijuana into their treatment practices. Dr. Mark Wallace, who chairs the division of pain medicine at the University of California–San Diego, has used marijuana to help several hundred patients transition off opioid painkillers. He says his patients tell him, "I feel like I was a slave to that drug [opioids]. I feel like I have my life back."[74]

As of 2018 twenty-nine states and the District of Columbia recognize the benefit of medical marijuana and have made it legal. However, to effectively fight the opioid crisis, the government must decriminalize marijuana on a federal level, encourage research and development of new drugs based on the marijuana plant, and empower doctors to legally prescribe medical marijuana to their patients.

Medical Marijuana Will Not Prevent Opioid Abuse

"I am astonished to hear people suggest that we can solve our heroin crisis by legalizing marijuana, so people can trade one life-wrecking dependency for another."

—Jeff Sessions, attorney general of the United States

Quoted in Reuters, "Legalized Marijuana Could Help Curb the Opioid Epidemic, Study Finds," NBC News, March 27, 2017. www.nbcnews.com.

Consider these questions as you read:

1. Taking into account the facts and ideas presented in this discussion, how persuasive is the argument that marijuana is dangerous for teens? Which reasons are strongest and why?
2. Has this essay convinced you that marijuana is a gateway drug? Why or why not?
3. The essay makes the argument that legalizing marijuana without properly studying its risks is similar to the way doctors liberally prescribed opioids without understanding their potential for abuse. How are the situations similar, and how are they different?

Editor's note: The discussion that follows presents common arguments made in support of this perspective, reinforced by facts, quotes, and examples taken from various sources.

Marijuana is classified as a Schedule I drug under the Controlled Substances Act. This means that the DEA has determined that marijuana has no medical value and a high potential for abuse. Yet state after state has legalized marijuana for medical—and in some cases recreational—purposes, flooding the country with extremely potent strains of the drug. If the hype surrounding medical marijuana is to be believed, it is the holy grail of medicines: a safe, effective, nonaddictive cure for almost any ill—including the opioid epidemic.

Marijuana is none of these things. It is far from harmless—especially for teenagers with developing brains. It is also an addictive gateway drug to opioids, priming teen brains to be more susceptible to opioid addiction. Yet young people are getting the message that marijuana is a safe alternative to opioids. This is simply untrue. Easy access to marijuana is not an answer to the opioid crisis. Instead, it will only encourage more abuse and addiction.

Marijuana Stunts the Teen Brain

Many people assume that because marijuana is a plant, it is a natural substance and therefore not harmful. This is not true. Marijuana use can cause permanent damage to the developing brain—especially to those regions responsible for impulse control and making sound decisions, such as avoiding drugs like opioids. The prefrontal cortex—the part of the brain that regulates higher-level thinking and decision making—is not fully developed in humans until age twenty-five. During the teen and young adult years, the brain prunes away neural connections that are no longer useful. Brain studies have demonstrated that marijuana can stop this pruning process, which makes it harder to think clearly and resist impulses.

In addition, an August 2012 study published in the journal *Proceedings of the National Academy of Sciences of the United States of America* found that people who used marijuana as teens experienced a decline in IQ by the time they were thirty-eight years old—even if they stopped using marijuana as adults. According to Dr. Nassima Ait-Daoud Tiouririne of the University of Virginia, "Since marijuana use impairs critical cognitive functions, both during acute intoxication and days after use, many students could be functioning at a cognitive level that is below their natural ability for considerable periods of time." She says this can cause a "snowball effect" of failures, "with one failure leading to many."[75] Tiouririne notes that research has shown that teens who use marijuana daily are 60 percent less likely to get their high school diploma than those who have never used marijuana, 2.3 times more likely to drop out, and 8

Marijuana Is a Gateway Drug to Opioids

Using marijuana increases one's risk of abusing opioids, according to a 2018 study that examined the substance abuse patterns of US adults. The study found that those who used marijuana at the start of the study, whether to relieve pain or recreationally, were more likely to abuse opioids three years later than nonusers of marijuana. It also found that the more frequently participants used marijuana, the more likely they were to abuse opioids. This supports the idea that marijuana is a gateway drug to illicit opioid use.

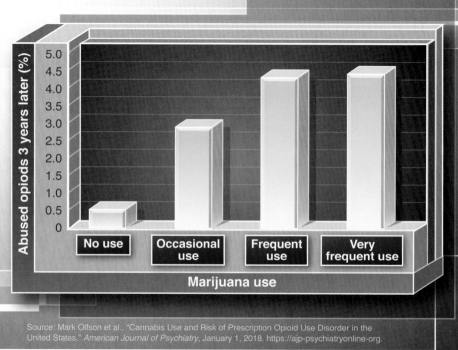

Source: Mark Olfson et al., "Cannabis Use and Risk of Prescription Opioid Use Disorder in the United States," *American Journal of Psychiatry*, January 1, 2018. https://ajp-psychiatryonline-org.

times more likely to make poor decisions that cause them to use dangerous drugs like opioids.

Marijuana can also cause mental disorders—especially in teens. People with mental disorders are at much higher risk of using opioids as adults. A 2017 study published in the *Journal of the American Board of Family Medicine* found that the 16 percent of Americans who have mental disorders receive over half of all opioids prescribed in the United States. Studies have shown that teens who smoke marijuana are more likely to develop psychotic disorders such as schizophrenia. In a study of adults with schizophrenia presented at the World Psychiatric Association's World Congress of Psychiatry in Berlin in 2017, researchers found that using marijuana before age eighteen hastened the onset of the disease by ten years.

Meanwhile, other studies link teen marijuana use to depression and anxiety. The increase in risk is related to the high THC content (the psychoactive chemical that causes people to experience a high) in today's marijuana strains. THC disrupts the body's natural endocannabinoid system and can lead to depression and anxiety. "Too little endocannabinoid signaling . . . can promote anxiety disorders," says neuroscientist R. Douglas Fields. "Too much activity has the opposite effect and can promote depression."[76]

Marijuana Is Addictive and Primes the Brain for Opioids

Marijuana is especially addictive to the teenaged brain. "Because the brain is so adaptable while it's still developing, it's highly susceptible to dependencies, even from non-opioids such as today's newly potent marijuana strains,"[77] writes US Admiral James Winnefeld, who lost his son to a heroin overdose. Winnefeld's son used marijuana at an early age and developed various addictions before moving on to opioids. According to Tiouririne, 30 percent of those who use marijuana have some level of addiction to the substance, and people who start using the drug before age eighteen are four to seven times more likely to develop dependence and addiction issues.

Also, as Winnefeld writes, recent research has shown that because marijuana is addictive, it "prepares the brain to be receptive to opioids."[78] For instance, a 2014 study published in *European Neuropsychopharmacology* confirmed early studies that found that adolescent rats exposed to THC exhibited more heroin-seeking

> "Because the brain is so adaptable while it's still developing, it's highly susceptible to dependencies, even from non-opioids such as today's newly potent marijuana strains."[77]
>
> —Admiral James Winnefeld

behavior later in life. And, according to psychologist David Fergusson, an analysis of data from his thirty-five-year-long population study "clearly suggest[s] the existence of some kind of causative association in which the use of cannabis increases the likelihood that the user will go on to use other illicit drugs."[79]

Scientists have found that marijuana primes the brain for opioid addiction by making it less sensitive to dopamine—the brain chemical involved in learning and reward. People less sensitive to dopamine tend to be thrill seekers; they need far more stimulation to experience a sense of reward. They also are drawn to powerful psychoactive drugs like opioids that artificially create feelings of euphoria. In short, drugs like opioids are so rewarding to people with low dopamine that they become addicted to the drugs more easily. Their brains compel them to seek out the drug, even though it is destroying their lives.

Admiral Winnefeld's son, Jonathan, was a victim of the gateway drug phenomenon. Jonathan used marijuana in his early teens as a way to self-medicate for undiagnosed depression and anxiety, but his drug use only exacerbated his mental illness. He quickly moved from marijuana to more powerful prescription drugs, including opioids. His parents helped him through sixteen months of rehab, but he could not resist the pull of his addiction and overdosed during his first week of college. "Jonathan was very serious about his recovery," Winnefeld writes. "He fought honorably against the demons of this disease, but, as with so many others, he lost his battle."[80] Thousands of young people have died the same way, and more are dying every day. According to the CDC, from 2015 to 2016, drug overdose deaths increased by 28 percent among fifteen- to twenty-four-year-olds—many of whom had easy access to today's powerful strains of marijuana.

Repeating the Opioid Crisis

Marijuana is not approved by the FDA because there have been no large-scale, controlled clinical trials that establish its safety and effectiveness. This means that states that have legalized medical marijuana are essentially encouraging their citizens to participate in an unregulated experiment with an addictive psychoactive drug. This is uncomfortably similar to the situation several decades ago that caused the opioid crisis. According to the Trump administration's 2017 report on the opioid crisis, the rush to recommend medical marijuana to patients without a clear understanding of its risks "mirrors the lack of data in the 1990s and early 2000s when opioid prescribing multiplied across health care settings and led to the current epidemic of abuse, misuse and addiction."[81] In other words, the same situation that resulted in overprescribing opioids is being repeated. As more states send the message that marijuana is safe and nonaddictive, as more doctors recommend it, and as more people self-medicate with it, teens are getting the message that it is safe and nonaddictive to use recreationally.

> "The use of cannabis increases the likelihood that the user will go on to use other illicit drugs."[79]
>
> —Psychologist David Fergusson

The push for legalization of medical marijuana has flooded the United States with cheap, high-potency strains of the drug. And just as teens once raided their parents' medicine cabinets for prescription opioids—exposure that led to an epidemic of heroin addiction and overdose—today's young people can easily acquire powerful strains of medical marijuana to use recreationally. This has the potential to prime thousands of young people for opioid addiction. Marijuana will not solve the opioid crisis—it can only make it worse.

Source Notes

Overview: Opioid Abuse

1. Quoted in Katharine Seelye, "1 Son, 4 Overdoses, 6 Hours," *New York Times*, January 21, 2018. https://mobile.nytimes.com.
2. Quoted in Seelye, "1 Son, 4 Overdoses, 6 Hours."
3. Quoted in Jerry Mitchell, "With 175 Americans Dying a Day, What Are the Solutions to the Opioid Epidemic?," *USA Today*, January 29, 2018. www.usatoday.com.
4. Christopher Caldwell, "American Carnage," *First Things*, April 2017. www.firstthings.com.
5. Caldwell, "American Carnage."
6. Matt Ganem, *The Science of Opioid Withdrawal*, YouTube, May 27, 2016. www.youtube.com/watch?v=CduCr-kJXtk.
7. Ganem, *The Science of Opioid Withdrawal*.
8. Stacy Seikel, "Distinguishing Between Pain-Related Dependence and Addiction," RiverMend Health. www.rivermendhealth.com.
9. Quoted in Alice Park, "Life After Addiction," *Time*, October 15, 2017. http://time.com.

Chapter One: Should Opioids Be Used to Treat Chronic Pain?

10. John Nolte, "The Other Side of the Opioid Debate—the Individual," Daily Wire, March 30, 2017. www.dailywire.com.
11. Quoted in Page Leggett, "Opioid Overview," *PainPathways Magazine*, September 1, 2015. www.painpathways.org.
12. iPain, "iPain Media Press Sheet," 2016. https://powerofpain.org.
13. Jeffrey Singer, "The Myth of an Opioid Prescription Crisis," Cato Institute, 2017. www.cato.org.
14. Nora D. Volkow and A. Thomas McLellan, "Opioid Abuse in Chronic Pain—Misconceptions and Mitigation Strategies," *New England Journal of Medicine*, March 31, 2016. www.nejm.org.
15. iPain, "iPain Media Press Sheet."
16. International Association for the Study of Pain, "EFIC's Declaration on Chronic Pain as a Major Healthcare Problem, a Disease in Its Own Right," 2001. https://s3.amazonaws.com.

17. Quoted in Kate Masters, "Chronic Pain Patients Report Struggles Under Tighter Opioid Regulations," *Frederick (MD) News-Post*, February 12, 2018. www.fredericknewspost.com.

18. Quoted in Masters, "Chronic Pain Patients Report Struggles Under Tighter Opioid Regulations."

19. Jacqueline, personal communication with the author, January 26, 2018.

20. Quoted in Sondra, personal communication with the author, January 28, 2018.

21. Sam Quinones, *Dreamland: The True Tale of America's Opiate Epidemic*. London: Bloomsbury, 2015, p. 291. Kindle edition.

22. Antonia F. Chen, Jane C. Ballantyne, and Meghna Patel, "Point/Counterpoint: Opioid Abuse in the United States," *Healthcare Transformation*, March 1, 2017. www.liebertpub.com.

23. Quoted in Kaiser Health News, "Jury's In: Opioids Are Not Better than Other Medicines for Chronic Pain," NBC News, March 7, 2018. www.nbcnews.com.

24. Quoted in Kelly Servick, "Why Painkillers Sometimes Make the Pain Worse," *Science*, November 3, 2016. www.sciencemag.org.

25. Quoted in Servick, "Why Painkillers Sometimes Make the Pain Worse."

26. Murray McAllister, "Six Common Assumptions in the Opioid Management Debate," Institute for Chronic Pain, September 20, 2015. www.instituteforchronicpain.org.

27. McAllister, "Six Common Assumptions in the Opioid Management Debate."

28. McAllister, "Six Common Assumptions in the Opioid Management Debate."

29. Quoted in Associated Press, "Prescription Opioids Fail Rigorous New Test for Chronic Pain," *STAT*, March 6, 2018. www.statnews.com.

Chapter Two: Who Is Responsible for the Opioid Epidemic?

30. Art Van Zee, "The Promotion and Marketing of OxyContin: Commercial Triumph, Public Health Tragedy," *American Journal of Public Health*, February 2009. www.ncbi.nlm.nih.gov.

31. John Temple, *American Pain*. Guilford, CT: Lyons, 2016, p. 43.

32. Quoted in Harriet Ryan et al., "'You Want a Description of Hell?' OxyContin's 12-Hour Problem," *Los Angeles Times*, May 5, 2016. www.latimes.com.

33. Quoted in Ryan et al., "You Want a Description of Hell?"

34. Quoted in Ryan et al., "You Want a Description of Hell?"

35. Quoted in Patrick Keefe, "The Family That Built an Empire of Pain," *New Yorker*, October 30, 2017. www.newyorker.com.
36. Quoted in "How Corporate Greed Helped Create the Current Opioid Addiction Crisis," *Daily Kos* (blog), May 2, 2017. www.dailykos.com.
37. Quoted in Ryan et al., "You Want a Description of Hell?"
38. Quoted in Keefe, "The Family That Built an Empire of Pain."
39. State of California, Assembly Bill No. 507, Chapter 396 (filed October 2, 2011). https://leginfo.legislature.ca.gov.
40. Quoted in Jenn Karlman, "Timeline: How Prescription Drugs Became a National Crisis," Fox 5, February 16, 2017. http://fox5sandiego.com.
41. John Gray, "HDA Statement on Misreporting by the *Washington Post* on Distributors, Opioid Epidemic," Healthcare Distribution Alliance, December 15, 2017. www.healthcaredistribution.org.
42. John Hammergren, "Let's Shine Real Light on the Opioid Crisis—and What to Do About It," *Washington Post*, December 22, 2017. www.washingtonpost.com.
43. Glenn Simon, "The Opioid Crisis Can't Be Blamed on Big Pharma Alone," *National Review*, September 20, 2017. www.nationalreview.com.
44. Caldwell, "American Carnage."
45. Simon, "The Opioid Crisis Can't Be Blamed on Big Pharma Alone."
46. Quoted in German Lopez, "America's Huge Problem with Opioid Prescribing, in One Quote," Vox, September 18, 2017. www.vox.com.
47. Art Levine, "How the VA Fueled the National Opioid Crisis and Is Killing Thousands of Veterans," *Newsweek*, October 12, 2017. www.newsweek.com.
48. Quoted in Jim Axelrod, "Veterans Dying from Overmedication," CBS News, September 19, 2013. www.cbsnews.com.

Chapter Three: Can Regulating Opioid Prescriptions More Strictly Prevent Their Abuse?

49. Ross White, personal communication with the author, January 28, 2018.
50. Quoted in Jessica Wapner, "CDC Study Finds Opioid Dependency Begins Within a Few Days of Initial Use," *Newsweek*, March 22, 2017. www.newsweek.com.
51. Centers for Disease Control and Prevention, *Guidelines for Prescribing Opioids for Chronic Pain*, March 15, 2016. www.cdc.gov.
52. Quoted in *All Things Considered*, "Opioid Prescriptions Falling but Remain Too High, CDC Says," National Public Radio, July 6, 2017. www.npr.org.
53. Chen, Ballantyne, and Patel, "Point/Counterpoint."
54. Centers for Disease Control and Prevention, "Vital Signs: Changes in Opioid Prescribing in the United States, 2006–2015," 2017. www.cdc.gov.

55. Chen, Ballantyne, and Patel, "Point/Counterpoint."
56. Quoted in Richard Blumenthal, United States Senator for Connecticut, "Blumenthal, Markey, Warren, Feinstein, & Manchin Call for Mandatory Education for Prescribers of Opioids," July 14, 2017. www.blumenthal.senate.gov.
57. Terri Lewis, "The States of Pain Regulation: What About Discharge & Follow-Up?," *Diseases & Conditions* (blog), National Pain Report, September 22, 2017. http://nationalpainreport.com.
58. Singer, "The Myth of an Opioid Prescription Crisis."
59. Lynn Webster, "The DEA Raids the Offices of My Friend and Colleague, Dr. Tennant," *The Painful Truth* (blog), November 18, 2017. http://the painfultruthbook.com.
60. Quoted in Pat Anson, "DEA Raids Dr. Forest Tennant's Pain Clinic," Pain News Network, November 16, 2017. www.painnewsnetwork.org.
61. Singer, "The Myth of an Opioid Prescription Crisis."
62. Susan Glod, "The Other Victims of the Opioid Epidemic," *New England Journal of Medicine*, June 1, 2017. www.nejm.org.
63. Quoted in Anson, "DEA Raids Dr. Forest Tennant's Pain Clinic."
64. Michelle, comment on Pat Anson, "DEA Cutting Rx Opioid Supply in 2018," Pain News Network, November 10, 2017. www.painnewsnetwork.org.
65. Singer, "The Myth of an Opioid Prescription Crisis."

Chapter Four: Can Medical Marijuana Prevent Opioid Abuse?

66. National Cannabis Industry Association, *Cannabis: A Promising Option for the Opioid Crisis*, 2016. http://thecannabisindustry.org.
67. Eric P. Baron, "Comprehensive Review of Medicinal Marijuana, Cannabinoids, and Therapeutic Implications in Medicine and Headache: What a Long Strange Trip It's Been," *Headache*, June 1, 2015, p. 890.
68. Quoted in Minnesota Department of Health, "Intractable Pain Patients in the Minnesota Medical Cannabis Program: Experience of Enrollees During the First Five Months," March 6, 2018. www.health.state.mn.us.
69. Quoted in National Cannabis Industry Association, *Cannabis*.
70. Quoted in National Cannabis Industry Association, *Cannabis*.
71. Quoted in National Cannabis Industry Association, *Cannabis*.

72. Melvin Livingston et al., "Recreational Cannabis Legalization and Opioid-Related Deaths in Colorado, 2000–2015," *American Journal of Public Health*, November 2017. http://ajph.aphapublications.org.proxy .library.vcu.edu.

73. Quoted in Matt Richtel, "Addiction Specialists Ponder a Potential Aid: Pot," *New York Times*, March 27, 2017. www.nytimes.com.

74. Quoted in Richtel, "Addiction Specialists Ponder a Potential Aid."

75. Nassima Ait-Daoud Tiouririne, "A Review on Medical Marijuana," Slide-Player, 2015. http://slideplayer.com.

76. R. Douglas Fields, "Link Between Adolescent Pot Smoking and Psychosis Strengthens," *Scientific American*, October 20, 2017. www.scientificameri can.com.

77. James Winnefeld, "No Family Is Safe from This Epidemic," *Atlantic*, November 29, 2017. www.theatlantic.com.

78. Winnefeld, "No Family Is Safe from This Epidemic."

79. Quoted in Dave Levitan, "Is Marijuana Really a 'Gateway Drug'?," Fact-Check.org, April 23, 2015. www.factcheck.org.

80. Winnefeld, "No Family Is Safe from This Epidemic."

81. President's Commission on Combating Drug Addiction and the Opioid Crisis, *Final Report*, 2017. www.whitehouse.gov.

Opioid Abuse Facts

Opioid Overdose

- According to the Substance Abuse and Mental Health Services Administration, 115 Americans died every day from an opioid overdose in 2016, a rate five times higher than in 1999. In total, more than 630,000 people died from drug overdose from 1999 to 2016.
- In 2016, 15,469 people died from heroin overdose and 19,413 people died from fentanyl overdose, according to the US Department of Health and Human Services.
- The CDC reports that emergency room visits for opioid overdoses increased 30 percent in forty-five states from July 2016 to September 2017. In metropolitan areas, the number of visits grew by 54 percent.
- According to the health care group CO*RE, in 2016 drug overdose deaths rose 50 percent among twenty-five- to thirty-four-year-olds.
- The National Vital Statistics System found that in 2016 life expectancy in the United States fell for the second year in a row due to an increase in deaths from opioid overdose.

Hard-Hit States

- The American Enterprise Institute found that West Virginia spends $4,378 per resident on the opioid epidemic, followed by Washington, DC, ($3,657); New Hampshire ($3,640); and Ohio ($3,385).
- According to the *New York Times*, one-tenth of New Hampshire residents are addicted to drugs.
- A congressional investigation found that pharmaceutical distributing companies shipped nearly 21 million opioid painkillers to two pharmacies in Williamson, West Virginia, from 2006 to 2016. Williamson has a population of twenty-nine hundred.

- According to *U.S. News & World Report*, heroin-related overdoses in West Virginia have increased by 200 percent since regulations to limit opioid prescribing were put in place.
- According to the DEA website Just Think Twice, one in five high school seniors in West Virginia say they know how to get heroin easily.

Teen Opioid Abuse

- The US Department of Health and Human Services reports that 3.6 percent of youths aged twelve to seventeen said they misused opioids in 2016.
- According to the website Addiction Hope, 65 percent of teens say that home medicine cabinets are their source of drugs, and 50 percent believe these drugs are safer than illegal street drugs.
- According to a 2017 study published in *Pediatrics*, most teens who abuse opioids were first prescribed them by a doctor.
- The National Institute on Drug Abuse states that out of every ten teens who abuse opioids, seven mix them with other drugs like alcohol (52.1 percent) and marijuana (58.5 percent), greatly increasing their chance of fatal overdose.
- The CDC estimates that for every teen or young adult overdose death, there are 119 emergency room visits and twenty-two treatment admissions.

Doctor Prescribing

- The *Annual Surveillance Report of Drug-Related Risks and Outcomes* states that in 2016 doctors wrote 66.5 opioid prescriptions for every 100 persons. About 1 in 5 people received 1 or more opioid prescriptions, with the average patient receiving 3.5 prescriptions.
- A 2016 survey by the National Safety Council found that 99 percent of doctors prescribe opioids for longer than the three days recommended by the CDC, and 23 percent prescribe at least a month's worth at a time.

- The survey also found that only 38 percent of doctors who see evidence of opioid abuse refer their patients to treatment, and only 5 percent are willing to treat them for opioid abuse themselves.

Opioid Treatment

- Experts estimate that only one in ten people addicted to opioids seeks treatment.
- According to the website DrugAbuse.com, 91 percent of those in recovery for opioid addiction will experience a relapse, 59 percent relapse in the first week of sobriety, and 80 percent relapse within a month.

Related Organizations and Websites

Centers for Disease Control and Prevention (CDC)
1600 Clifton Rd.
Atlanta, GA 30329
website: www.cdc.gov

The CDC is the federal agency charged with protecting public health and safety from disease, including addiction. Its web page on opioids contains information about the opioid epidemic, overdose prevention, and links to various studies and statistics.

Drug Enforcement Administration (DEA)
800 K St. NW, Suite 500
Washington, DC 20001
website: www.dea.gov

The DEA is a law enforcement agency that enforces laws related to controlled substances like opioids. Its website contains fact sheets and other information on opioids such as OxyContin, heroin, and fentanyl, as well as various news reports and press releases related to opioids.

National Institute on Drug Abuse (NIDA)
6001 Executive Blvd.
Room 5213, MSC 9561
Bethesda, MD 20892
website: www.drugabuse.gov

NIDA is a government organization that conducts and disseminates research on drug use and addiction. Its web page on opioids contains general information on opioids and opioid abuse and links to national surveys and other statistics.

Operation Prevention

website: www.operationprevention.com

Operation Prevention is an organization that educates young people, in schools and online, about opioid addiction. Its website contains various activities and videos, including e-learning modules and a virtual field trip.

Pain News Network

2708 Foothill Blvd. #261
La Crescenta, CA 91214
website: www.painnewsnetwork.org

The Pain News Network is a nonprofit online news service that provides in-depth coverage about chronic pain and pain management. Its website contains hundreds of articles related to opioids and the treatment of chronic pain.

Substance Abuse and Mental Health Services Administration (SAMHSA)

5600 Fishers Ln.
Rockville, MD 20857
website: www.samhsa.gov

SAMHSA is a federal agency that leads public health efforts to reduce substance abuse and its impact on communities. Its web page on opioids includes information on opioid addiction, statistics, and links to national surveys.

US Department of Health and Human Services (HHS)

200 Independence Ave. SW
Washington, DC 20201
website: www.hhs.gov

The HHS is the federal agency charged with protecting the health and well-being of Americans. Its website contains a section on the national opioid crisis and includes a wealth of information about the epidemic, prevention, treatment, and recovery.

For Further Research

Books

Johann Hari, *Chasing the Scream: The First and Last Days of the War on Drugs*. London: Bloomsbury, 2016.

Anna Lembke, *Drug Dealer, MD: How Doctors Were Duped, Patients Got Hooked, and Why It's So Hard to Stop*. Baltimore: Johns Hopkins University Press, 2016.

Barry Meier, *Pain Killer: An Empire of Deceit and the Origin of America's Opioid Epidemic*. New York: Random House, 2018.

Sam Quinones, *Dreamland: The True Tale of America's Opiate Epidemic*. London: Bloomsbury, 2015. Kindle edition.

John Temple, *American Pain: How a Young Felon and His Ring of Doctors Unleashed America's Deadliest Drug Epidemic*. Guilford, CT: Lyons, 2016.

Internet Sources

Christopher Caldwell, "American Carnage," *First Things*, April 2017. www.firstthings.com/article/2017/04/american-carnage.

Centers for Disease Control and Prevention, *Guidelines for Prescribing Opioids for Chronic Pain*, 2016. www.cdc.gov/drugoverdose/pdf/Guide lines_Factsheet-a.pdf.

Patrick Keefe, "The Family That Built an Empire of Pain," *New Yorker*, October 30, 2017. www.newyorker.com/magazine/2017/10/30/the -family-that-built-an-empire-of-pain.

Art Levine, "How the VA Fueled the National Opioid Crisis and Is Killing Thousands of Veterans," *Newsweek*, October 12, 2017. www.news week.com/2017/10/20/va-fueled-opioid-crisis-killing-veterans-681552 .html.

National Cannabis Industry Association, *Cannabis: A Promising Option for the Opioid Crisis*, 2016. http://thecannabisindustry.org/wp-content /uploads/2016/10/NCIA-Cannabis-and-Opioids-Report.October-2016 .pdf.

President's Commission on Combating Drug Addiction and the Opioid Crisis, Final Report, 2017. www.whitehouse.gov/sites/whitehouse.gov /files/images/Final_Report_Draft_11-1-2017.pdf.

Harriet Ryan, Lisa Girion, and Scott Glover, "'You Want a Description of Hell?' OxyContin's 12-Hour Problem," *Los Angeles Times*, May 5, 2016. www.latimes.com/projects/oxycontin-part1.

Jeffrey Singer, "The Myth of an Opioid Prescription Crisis," Cato Institute, September/October 2017. www.cato.org/policy-report/sept emberoctober-2017/myth-opioid-prescription-crisis.

Index

About the Author

Christine Wilcox writes fiction and nonfiction for young adults and adults. She has worked as an editor, an instructional designer, and a writing instructor. She lives in Richmond, Virginia, with her husband, David, and their son, Anthony.